THE
RHODESIAN
RIDGEBACK
TODAY

Stig G. Carlson

Howell Book House

New York

HOWELL BOOK HOUSE
IDG Books Worldwide, Inc.
An International Data Group Company
1633 Broadway
New York, NY 10019

Library of Congress Cataloging-in-Publication Data
Carlson, Stig G.
     The Rhodesian Ridgeback Today / Stig G. Carlson.
          p.   cm.
     Includes index.
     ISBN 1-58245-039-0
     1. Rhodesian ridgeback.   I. Title.
SF429.R5C37   1999
636.753'6--dc21   98-34966
                                          CIP

Manufactured in Singapore

10 9 8 7 6 5 4 3 2 1

ACKNOWLEDGEMENTS

There is a saying that "Disillusion comes from learning from your own mistakes, Experience comes from mistakes made by others". My wife Bea has supported me, through what became an 18-month process, by keeping my focus on strengths and positive experience, rather than negative ones. Also, she has helped me take a broad look at what the benefits of reading this book could be for a broad audience of dog lovers, Ridgeback owners, show enthusiasts, as well as breeders and judges.

It is impossible to list all the people or clubs that have contributed to this book. I am especially indebted to Katja Vogelsinger, the superb Austrian photographer, as well as Susan Clayborough in Norway, who provided both great photos and information. My artist daughter Sandra pushed me to dig into African nature and the RR history. My inspiration from the other side of the Atlantic came much thanks to Mrs Ulla-Britt Ekengren and Dr Pamela Rosman, who showed a never-ending willingness to help. Many a small club in "New Europe" has proven mature and helpful. Among clubs, I especially thank the German RRCD, which even invested in a 1600km drive just to make sure I got what I needed – and when. My friends and publishers at Ringpress deserve a lot of gratitude for their flexibility and creativity. Not least knowing that, in the end, I had a mix of too much and too little in data, plus a huge wealth of illustrations we needed to sort out.

Finally, I will always remember my old war-horse Lance, nearing 9 1/2 towards the end of this project. He has slept by my feet during the entire writing process. Always, when either my back or my mind has gone numb, he has been ready for a refreshing biking tour.

All photographs, unless stated otherwise, are by the author.

The future of the Ridgeback lies in the hands of responsible and imaginative breeders.
Picture courtesy: Linda Wooden, Norway

CONTENTS

INTRODUCTION

Those who have attended the Ridgeback World Congresses, which have been held every fourth year since 1984, know that there is no substitute for getting together, talking, exchanging views, listening and learning. The World Congresses would not have existed without the inspired work of two people, Liz and Brian Meggison of South Africa, and the future Rhodesian Ridgeback world is indebted to them for this pioneering work.

Back in 1922 a group of enthusiasts led by Francis Richard Barnes, plus a number of ridged dogs of all shapes, sizes and colours, gave birth to the idea of creating a breed out of ridged canines. In Johannesburg, in 1984, the first step was taken towards making the Rhodesian Ridgeback into a breed that would be recognised, honoured and admired throughout the world. We are not there yet. But my ambition, in writing this book, has been to see where we are today, and how broad the distribution of our breed is.

With the energetic assistance of my wife Bea I have communicated with over 130 countries to find out more about Rhodesian Ridgebacks, and I have come to realise the value of all types of infomation.

My hope is that the liberal use of photographs will form the very heart of this book. Hence I have taken the liberty of commenting on many of the pictures. Naturally this is a subjective, personal perspective. The real value, in the end, is what you, the reader, will take out and learn from the illustrations.

To put the breed into an historical perspective, it is important to remember that the Ridgeback is an African dog, with characteristics originating from long ago. However, in terms of appearance, it may be considered to be relatively recent in its development. This should not shock you. Many breeds that we think have always been around owe much to modern breeding. For example, the St Hubert, or Bloodhound, got its name from the descendants of William the Conqueror who named it 'the true (or pure) blood', but the breed as we know it today only emerged in the latter part of the 19th century.

Dog shows started over 150 years ago. No doubt, the explosion of breed-specific interest that grew out of this, starting in the UK, then in France and the US, followed by other countries, influenced a growing enthusiasm for finding indigenous breeds. The African continent was explored, and the Rhodesian Ridgeback was discovered.

Introduction

A breed in its own right, with its roots and its history in Africa, it is essential that this special identity is protected and preserved. It is equally important that other ridged dogs, such as the Thai Ridgeback, should be given a more appropriate name, such as the Thai Ridged Spitz, or Thai Ridged Dog. They are *not* close relatives to the Rhodesian Ridgeback.

Another significant and morally unavoidable issue is: who carries the responsibility for planning sound and specialised breeding programmes to ensure the future of the Ridgeback? The answer is clear and uncompromising. The responsibility for learning about the breed, for increasing understanding and for sharing this experience, lies with each and everyone of us. Clubs are catalysts; they are made up of members who are committed to their breed and they all carry a personal responsibility. No club structure should ever be allowed to take over individual responsibilities or individual rights. Neither should any club neglect, or even work contrary to, the members' ideas and wishes.

All clubs, as well as individual breeders, accumulate knowledge. Some countries approach the Ridgeback systematically, thanks to experienced RR clubs with a broad base of dogs to look at, others seem to have that fingertip feeling that is so essential to successful breeding. One of the many aspects of the Ridgeback is its versatility, and it has been a pleasure to receive information, suggestions, hints, even anecdotes, covering the many different disciplines. Anyone who wants to learn more about the Ridgeback is well-served by new material, whether it is about health statistics, lure coursing, agility training, obedience work or the show ring.

It is every owner's undeniable right to have his or her own dreams. The Parent Club in Harare, Zimbabwe, and its leaders, the Wallace family, has long personified the roots of the Rhodesian Ridgeback. Together with the breed and kennel clubs in Southern Africa, they form our threads that go back to the very beginnings of the breed. The bridge to the future is with you, the Ridgeback enthusiast. I hope that this book will be a building block in this bridge and that we can look forward to an ever-strengthening Rhodesian Ridgeback world in more and more countries.

Stig G. Carlson.

The Rhodesian Ridgeback's roots lie deep in Africa, but its development as a breed in its own right has been a relatively recent phenomenon.

Photo: T. Morgan.

1 HISTORY OF THE RHODESIAN RIDGEBACK

The Rhodesian Ridgeback as a formally defined breed of dog dates back only to the early 1920s, though its ancestry is rooted in the obscurity of past centuries. Since the birth of the Ridgeback as a recognised breed, much has been said and much has been speculated on, regarding the origin of the dog.

The Rhodesian Ridgeback is a breed of mixed ancestry, as are so many other of today's purebred dogs. One can claim that, at the year of writing these lines, the breed is three-quarters of a century old – which does not, by any means, make it a uniquely young breed. Even if hunting dogs, used more or less systematically in organised societies, date back to the Middle Ages, many of our modern hunting breeds are rather new. The functions of today's hunting companions developed in parallel with the developments of firearms for hunting.

The first 'breeding clubs' for dogs, for the lack of a better name, were formed in Europe in the 1860s. An example of the deliberate development of functional hunting dogs is the Pointer family, carrying British, French, Portuguese, Italian and, presumably, a fair amount of Spanish bird dog blood. From other breed groups, the Airedale terrier saw the light of day in the mid-19th century, and the Dobermann was launched towards the end of that century.

RIDGEBACK ORIGINS

If we establish that the birthplace of today's Ridgeback is the Southern African area, we can start the search for its origins with the original inhabitants of that region, the San people (also called Bushmen). Little is known about their early history, except that they were hunting and gathering tribes. Around two millennia ago, another tribe, the Khoikhoi (the alternative spelling is Xoixhoi), intruded on the Sans. The Khoikhoi brought with them sheep as domestic animals, but excavations suggest that neither of these early tribes had domesticated dogs. Then, again, this is a uncertain conclusion, as the domestication of dogs has been a long and gradual process, brought about by mutual benefits.

The wild canines which learnt that visiting human habitation meant food, also delivered the service of cleaning patrols, and early

'His history is of legend'.
Sandra Carlson.

warning systems. There is absolutely no reason to believe that the early canine partners of humans would have lived inside the human habitats, and hence skeletons are unlikely to be found close to human remains.

Canines did exist in Southern Africa in pre-historic days, for example jackals and the mysterious Lycaon pictus, or Cape Hunting dogs. Interestingly, Lycaon pictus has the same chromosome set-up as today's dogs, though it differs in many ways. There are scientists who claim that Cape Hunting dogs are not direct descendants of the wolf (*Canis lupus* family) but an older deviation from the ancestors which go back to the same original animals as for bears, cats, and dogs. Very recent studies of the Cape Hunting dogs, the most skilled and effective hunters among all mammals, and the second most endangered

species in Southern Africa, have started to change the perception of this caninoid. It has a strict social structure, it learns fast and carries lessons learnt over to at least seven or eight generations, and it is not the vicious killing machine that earlier literature has claimed. Legend or fiction – can this be part of the ancestry of the so-called 'Hottentot hunting dog', a special animal we have read about but have not been able to trace?

UNIQUE QUALITIES

Legends are born out of uniqueness. The real origin of Ridgebacks was the first group of dogs to carry a hair strip on their back. Eventually this strange hair formation caught people's eyes. Vasco da Gama is said to have encountered indigenous dogs, and there are claims that the Portuguese, by the dawn of the New Ages, had seen dog-like animals with strange hair formations. The same claims have been attributed to early Dutch sailors. Mrs Mylda Arsenis reported in her book about Ridged Dogs in Africa that the Austrian Professor Schulmuth, just before the Second World War, had found remains of well-preserved dogs in the mud layers of African rivers. These dogs had shown ridge-like formations of hair on their backs. Early names for these dogs, such as Verkeerdehaar (strange or crazy hair) or Maanhaar (mane hair) show that the vocabulary of the Africa-goers had noticed these canine peculiarities. I have myself seen, and obtained statuettes originating from the inner part of Western Central Africa, present-day Benin, which show symbolic hair formation on the backs of animals that must have reminded observers of strong Basenji-type dogs.

There are at least four other areas where ridged dogs have been found. There are the

Phu Quoc ridged dogs on an island off Vietnam. If they are the ancestor of today's 'Thai Ridgeback', then the breed that emerged should be called Thai Ridged Spitz – this is just a proposal! There have also been ridged canines in Cambodia, the 'Riscas' dogs in the old Portuguese island colony of Timor, and around the Tiger Bay area in present-day Angola.

THE PORTUGUESE OBSERVERS
Interestingly, we see a common denominator of Portuguese links in the above. A Portuguese poet and historian, Professor Vitorino Nemesio, has revealed how Portuguese caravels used dogs on board to keep rats away, as dogs could reach parts of the ships human beings could not. The Portuguese, the master seamen of the last decades of the Middle Ages and for years after that, are the only known seafarers to have carried dogs for other purposes than – possibly – taking them along as food.

The Persian Gulf and Arabic link, as a potential transport route for early ridged dogs from the Middle East or Asia to Africa, has always disturbed me. This theory falls down on the logic of why so few ridged dogs have survived in these areas, and also that these are people who have never, and still do not, value dogs as worthy animals and partners in their societies.

I quote below Mr Cesar M. de Castro Martines, a keen Portuguese traveller, researcher and breeder. With some luck, thanks to him, we might have some real, live Tiger Bay ridged dogs in Europe within a few years.

Mr Martines has paid special attention to the fact that the Portuguese seafarers used to stop for water and food in the Angolan area of Mocamedes before crossing the Indian Ocean. This is the country of the Kamussekeles tribe. The Kamussekeles form one of the four tribes of Namibe in Angola. They are of Khoikhoi origin, as are the Mukubaios and the Guenguelas. The fourth, the Kwanhamas, are warriors and shepherds of Zulu ancestry. Here are some notes from Mr. Martines:

During the 18th century there was an outbreak of rabies in the city of Mocamedes (present Namibia-Angola). The authorities ordered all dogs to be destroyed. Some animal lovers where shocked and responded by deciding to take their dogs to a place of no return.

A bumboat was turned into a veritable Noah's ark for dogs which were of all breeds ,shapes and sizes, both males and females, and including the dogs of the Kamussekeles. The Kamussekele dogs, the companions of these Khoikhoi people who live in the Namibian desert, the gateway to the great Kalahari, carry ridge formations on their backs.

The ship set sail and headed South looking for a safe area to leave their dogs. They reached the Tiger Bay peninsula, unloaded their dogs on the beaches and left them in hope they would survive.

There are, naturally, no records of what happened after this rescue attempt. But one can imagine the horror and the fierce struggle to survive. What we do know is that in spite of the drama that those unseen days must have witnessed, the surviving dogs adapted to the new harsh conditions of life, evolving into a new breed of dog – the robust, wild and brave Tiger Bay Dog. Some ninety per cent of these dogs carry a ridge on their backs, just like the Kamussekele dogs.

One can assume that in the beginning they must have realised that in order to survive they needed to form groups or packs. They learnt to quench their thirst by chewing crabs and by sticking their tongues out over the crest of the sea water absorbing the microscopic pearls of fresh water that hang on top as a result of evaporation. Perfecting these techniques made it possible for them to survive.

The dogs also found out that seals were a delicacy but that any animal was good to eat, including the fish that swam along the beach. They also learnt that they could not hunt the abundant albatrosses single-handed so they developed a group hunting technique. They realised that, due to its weight, the albatross has to run for several metres against the wind to take off. The dogs, having pinpointed their target, waited until two dogs had quickly swum out, positioning themselves up-wind and able to cut off the launching path of the bird. The albatrosses attack by trying to peck the eyes of the dogs, while the dogs feign a battle just to distract the prey. Meanwhile the real hunter, normally a bitch, attacks from behind, breaking the neck of the albatross.

These dogs still exist, as I have sighted them both in 1993 and 1995. Most of them are brindle, though you can also find golden red ones. The majority of these dogs have ridges.

Many conclusions can be drawn, not least about the dominance of the Ridge and the hunting abilities of the ridged dogs (I deliberately did not use the word Ridgeback). Were the Kamussekeles dogs the ancestors of the mixed groups of ridged dogs in Southern Africa? We will never know for sure. The early history is legend – but we can learn from legends as well.

HUNTING LION
Another reason why today's Ridgebacks deserve attention, interest and admiration is their proven hunting ability. We will look more in detail at these qualities in later chapters. There were many dogs that were capable hunters but destiny decided that one type should be preferred ahead of others – those who could also serve man in big game hunting.

Hunting the majestic prey of Africa and, above all, the killing of lions, was the ultimate sign of manhood before and after the turn of the 19th century. This brutal slaughter of wonderful wildlife can hardly be acceptable when viewed from our modern perspective, but in those days hunters became world-famous. Frederick Courtney Selous, possibly the most famous of them all, counted the US President, the German Kaiser and leading industrial magnates among his personal friends. Leading authors such as Rider Haggard, as well as Wilbur Smith, used him as a role model. Though we find this amazing today, especially if you have, as I have done, spent years working with the World-Wide Fund for Nature (WWF), we must accept that times change and we have to take historic reality for what it is.

It is unclear whether Selous consciously used hunting dogs with ridges. One of his foremost successors, Cornelius van Rooyen, did and for some time the Ridged dogs were even called 'van Rooyen's dogs'. Big game hunting made dog users in Southern Africa pay attention to ridged dogs because of their hunting abilities. Lion hunting created the fame which led to the use of the name 'the Lion Dog', a name that has done the breed some major and unfair disservice in Europe. More about this when we discuss temperament and Ridgebacks in modern society. Whether big game hunting is a virtue

'The African homeland.'
Sandra Carlson.

or a vice, the legendary reputation of those who were the hunter kings, hunting the King of Beasts, also reflected on the dogs they used. Out of these legends the modern Ridgeback was eventually born.

THE AFRICAN HOMELAND
Africa is, as we now know, the home of the oldest human developments, suggesting human beings evolved somewhere between Ethiopia and Tanzania. Hunting skills were probably developed between 20,000 and 60,000 years ago and hunting tools have been found both in the Tanzania region and in the Cape area. Early cave paintings were produced 20,000 years back in history in Namibia and soon after in Southern Africa. The use of ceramics and the planting of seeds were known as early as 7000 BC in

Northern Africa, cattle were kept in East Africa 3000 BC and iron production was mastered in Western Africa before 1000 BC. The area of present-day Mozambique exported iron products on a large scale from 100 AD and created the resources for the development of city-states in sub-equatorial Africa, for example in Zimbabwe.

Dogs developed alongside the human race long before the dawn of what we call history. Some archaeological findings date the earliest proven domestic dogs as being in Egypt about 7000 BC. If there were ridged dogs in those early days we do not know about them, and pictures in the early 20th century *Hutchinson's Dog Encyclopaedia*, showing a photo taken just before 1900 depicting three Sloughis carrying ridge-like formations, should not let the fantasy fly too far.

The early tribes of some 2000 years back, the Sans and the Khoikhois might have had a semi-detached relationship to canines in their environment.

TRIBAL MOVEMENTS
Around 500 BC the Bantu tribes started a movement towards the south. The Bantu cultures originally expanded out of present Nigeria between 3000 and 2000 BC. It is estimated that these Bantu-speaking tribes started to influence the southern tip of the African continent after the beginning of our era. Around 900 AD trade flourished between the East African ports and the Persian Gulf cultures. Mombassa became a shipping point for gold from Zimbabwe and, as early as the 15th century, this gold also reached Europe. The great Zimbabwe kingdom which existed about 1000 to 1400 AD produced city constructions that excite

admiration to this day. From the late 15th century, for some 200 years, the Portuguese dominated trade in East Africa and sailed the Indian Ocean.

There are Portuguese reports of having seen domestic dogs in South western Africa. Old missionary stories, it is claimed, have confirmed the existence of 'ridged dogs' in Africa. The Bantu movement southwards could have given the San and Khoikhoi tribes dogs, or even dogs with the hereditary qualities for ridge formations. Or, in theory, traders could have brought this mutation from the East. However, ridged dogs seem to have existed more in the Southwest than the East.

THE DEVELOPMENT OF THE CAPE
The Dutch, avoiding Portuguese naval stop-over locations on the Namibia side of Africa, established permanent settlements as service points for their trading ships in the Cape area. Jan van Riebeeck's landing there in 1652 marked the start of a Dutch colony. In parallel with this, as firearms developed in Europe, hunting became a new form of collecting food as well as a new pastime for the nobility.

The Dutch originally traded with the native people (often mixed together by them to be called Khoisan) but later ran into skirmishes about cattle and land. In the mid-18th century a new Dutch frontier was established, that of the border with the Bantu-speaking tribes, represented by the Xhosas.

We know for a fact that the Dutch brought along cattle and household animals. They also had strict instructions to learn quickly to use indigenous natural resources. Dogs no doubt were brought to Southern Africa. The most likely breeds in the early days of the settlements included various European hunting dogs, Bloodhound types, and probably also Mastiff-type dogs for guard purposes. At the same time the local tribes in the Southern African regions lived with domestic dogs.

The Cape areas soon saw an influx of immigrants from England and also from France, not least the Huguenots, and Dutch. In 1795 the British, then at war with France, landed in Southern Africa, eventually making the Cape province part of the Empire in 1814.

The areas south of the Limpopo saw the entry of new power brokers in the early 19th century in the shape of the magnificent Zulu warriors, led on this imperial quest by Shaka, the great Zulu commander. In what is now Zimbabwe, with links to the great Zimbabwe kingdom and the later Monomotapa kingdom, non-Zulu Shona-speaking people would soon meet parts of the Zulu tribes which split with the Zulu king. (In today's Zimbabwe some eighty per cent of the population are Shonas and sixteen per cent Ndebeles, that is of Zulu descent, and the rest are mostly white settlers.) The Zulus defeated the Nguni people in 1820. At the same time the British policies were felt to be increasingly oppressive by the Cape Dutch, causing some 15,000 men, women, children (and dogs) to flee their Cape homes and move north. The Boer movements and the Zulu migrations were in opposite directions. Bloody battles raged with the Southbound Zulus, who occasionally received British assistance. The decisive battle was at Blood River in December 1836, establishing what the Dutch Boers hoped would become a permanent homeland.

THE BOER REPUBLICS

Paintings, rugs, and also the reliefs at the Vortrekker Museum in Pretoria, show that the Boers were accompanied by their dogs. We do not have proof of any ridged dogs being particularly prominent but we do see the emergence of the other main use for 19th century dogs in Southern Africa, that of guards.

In the 1850s the Boers received independence in their Oranje and Transvaal Free States. Farming life developed to a stage which still exists today in some parts and which excludes the modern facilities of the electrical age. These were also the early days of what were known as the 'gold politics'. In 1888 Cecil Rhodes managed to sign a deal with the local king, Lobengula, creating a new state, soon to be known as Rhodesia. After two uprisings the local resistance was crushed by 1900. The Boers on the other hand did not accept British pressures and the Boer wars, between the British army and the freedom-loving Boers, took their terrible toll from 1899 to 1902. Lithographs of wagon trails and Boer defences show the presence of dogs.

Meanwhile the riches created by the gold, and the advances in communications, including fast steam ships, railways and also telegraphs and newspapers, brought an influx of people to Africa, and a global flow of news and information and more mobility to man – and, presumably, to man's dogs. These were the days when big game hunting emerged and the days when hunters and ridged dogs met for the first time.

DEVELOPMENT OF RHODESIA

While the Boer colonies were made Crown Colonies and, in 1910, were incorporated into the South African Union, life in the protectorate of Southern Rhodesia took its own course. In 1922 a group of keen dog people, inspired by the tales of hunters such as van Rooyen, gathered to discuss creating a breed out of the indigenous dogs, all of which were carrying ridges on their backs. This took place one year before Rhodesia became the independent Crown Colony of Southern Rhodesia. It was decided that the 'Son of Africa' would be the red-wheaten, agile, proud, strong and upstanding dog he is today. That decision was made at a farm in Bulawayo in present-day Zimbabwe

The Rhodesian Ridgeback of our age is a free-standing independent breed. It is not a breed to be compared with – or judged like – a Basenji or a Thai Ridged Spitz, for instance, but as the dog that has been born out of ages of development in Africa. Just as the Ridgeback is an independent breed, so is he also a Son of Africa.

Africa, the second largest continent, has sometimes been called the black continent. To me, Africa is the rainbow continent and, above all, the home of the blood-red sunsets, the warm reddish wheaten fields, the magic green jungles and the clear blue skies. The early history of Africa may be hidden in darkness but the environment that is the birthplace of the Ridgeback is the most colourful you could dream of. We can never know for sure what parts of the legends about the early Ridgeback are true, but every Ridgeback lover should take it as a task to visit the southern part of the African continent, walk the grass and sands, and smell the atmosphere of Africa. These are all part of the Ridgeback's legacy.

2 THE CHARACTER OF THE RIDGEBACK

"LION HEART AND FLYING PAWS"

The hunter halted his horse, and tried to look ahead into the dense bushland. The grass was man-high, the very early morning sun started to dry the dew from the ground. He looked back, noting that the carriers were not yet in sight. With a combined voice and hand signal he ordered the three dogs, which had easily followed his horse on the ride, into the vegetation ahead. He knew that less than a mile ahead was a watering place for big game. The dogs took off, making no noise.

The male lion was slowly walking away from the watering hole. He had eaten the previous evening and was not keen on hunting. Suddenly two dogs appeared, and the lion roared, more out of irritation than anger. The two dogs rapidly made attacking movements towards the rear of the lion, one from each side. The lion swivelled around, hitting out towards the nearest red-brownish menace with his paw. The dog was out of reach. The dog made another run towards the lion, again from behind, almost as the large lion paw had landed back on the ground. Suddenly, a third dog, greyish and ugly, appeared some distance

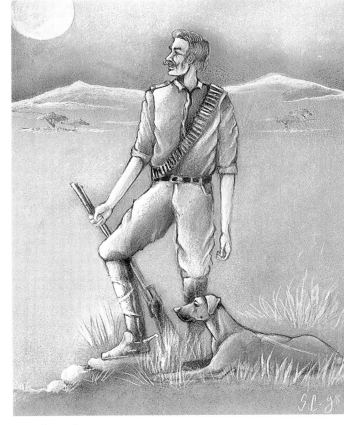

'Lionheart'.
Sandra Carlson.

'Flying paws'. Sandra Carlson.

in front of the lion, barking with a low, aggressive voice.

The two slender reddish-brown dogs, elegant in their feminine yet powerful movements, continued their seemingly random dance and their mock attacks against the lion's rear sides. The larger dog attempted to both attract attention and to create aggression by zigzagging in front of the lion. Suddenly a swift sweep from the lion's paw touched the flank of the bigger dog which rolled around, growling with pain. He got up and first started to limp away. But, seconds later, he continued his aggression, though from a greater distance.

In consternation, the lion stopped totally for a moment, only his head turning, as if to decide in which direction to mount a decisive attack. A single shot echoed out. The large lion fell slowly on its side, its legs buckling. The more slender dogs continued their strange dance around the animal, getting nearer, though not touching it. The larger, grey-coloured dog withdrew to lick his wound. The hunter's voice attracted the dogs, which somewhat reluctantly started to move gradually towards him as he came walking in. The dogs had again turned totally silent, but their bodies were still alert, almost vibrating from the excitement.

"THE NON-CONFRONTATIONAL GUARDIAN"

It was late fall, the Nordic darkness was total. Wet snow fell heavily from the sky. The young man walked along a narrow path, every now and then passing sparsely-placed lamp posts. The golden-brown dog followed half-reluctantly in the snow. The man did not keep the dog on a leash. Few people were awake close to midnight in this area and even fewer when the December weather turned really ugly.

The man suddenly halted, as he noticed that five or six people were hanging around in the area of the next light. In the snowstorm he had got within a few yards of them. Leather jackets gleamed in the faint light. One of the men turned to the walker and said something, which did not carry. The tone of voice was not totally friendly. Suddenly the dog pressed its side towards its owner, as if to force him to stand still, and then disappeared without a sound into the darkness. The dog owner still felt more curious than threatened.

The late night walker turned slightly to the right, to bypass the group of youngsters, which clearly at least wanted to challenge him to a talk. Some of the group members moved towards him, moving inside the light cone from the lamp. Suddenly, out of the darkness, in the direction of the dog owner, the face of the dog appeared, showing only a growling mouth and large, white teeth. The rest of the dog remained, half-lowered as if to jump, in the darkness. The growl was low and fierce.

The group of young men gathered closer,

16

almost as if to comfort each other. The dog took a tiny step forward and growled once more. Then they all backed off, moving, half-running, still throwing comments into the snowstorm, out of light and out of sight. The dog owner continued in the direction he had aimed at. "Come on, Douglas, enough now," he said, and the Ridgeback male slowly turned around, following his master. Once again the dog looked almost uninterested and continued its now silent, relaxed walk in the cold night.

SMART, SWIFT HUNTERS

Both those stories give a picture of typical Ridgeback behaviour. The hunting scene is fiction, based upon articles, letters and tales from old Africa. The modern little story is true in every detail.

The dogs that performed best in big game hunting were not the daredevils, the aggressive ones, nor the cowards that gave the game too much leeway. Many of these funny dogs with hair formations on their backs were noted for their exceptional swiftness, not least in sideways movements. They were also survivors; animals that could engage big game, keeping it at bay, and still avoiding the hostilities of the hunt.

The purebred Ridgeback of today still remains a true representative of its breed, possessing those wonderful qualities of bravery, caution and, above all, smartness and swiftness. Most stories from the big game hunts suggest that the females were the most agile and most skilled hunters. Quite naturally, there came, over time, a logical division of labour between females and males, with the latter gradually being seen as the perfect guardians, while still performing well in hunting.

One of the major challenges of breeding

'Perfect balance'. Sandra Carlson.

Ridgebacks for the twenty-first century is to learn even more about these breed-specific behavioural qualities, which made the breed so admired by African hunters.

It is a misconception that big game hunters used only ridged dogs. It is equally wrong to think that the ridged master hunters were only hunting lions. In the US, Ridgebacks have been used for cougar hunting; in Scandinavia there are reports about testing Ridgebacks in elk hunting, and in Africa when, in fact, performing more guarding than hunting duties, Ridgebacks are known to have faced different kinds of intruders on the farms. But in the end, despite the wonderfully natural guarding qualities of Ridgebacks, lion hunters, such as Lewis Christian, who is said to have killed more lions than any other known hunter, and R.H. Fraser, continued the tradition of using 'van Rooyen's dogs' in lion hunting. Hence many lions not only had to give their lives to the hunter and Ridgeback partnership, but also provided the breed with its claim to fame – 'the Kinghunters'.

THE NATURAL GUARDIAN

When looking at early documents about life in the southern African regions, we realise the enormous need for farm guardians that existed in those years of unrest and of extreme proximity to real wildlife. From among my numerous contacts, not least the tobacco-farming families in Southern Africa, many of whom are second or third generation farmers, it has been fascinating to hear how many people remember having grown up with ridged dogs. Some knowingly called them Ridgebacks – and most of them would never have another breed – while others talk about dogs with ridges. Two conclusions can be drawn from this.

First, that a true Ridgeback is a magnificent guard dog, with natural ability, an alert nature and tough enough to sort out threatening situations if the need arises. The Ridgeback is also known for being a non-violent guardsman, who seldom starts a fight unless it is necessary, who needs little or no guard training, and who can combine guarding qualities with being a wonderful family pet and the kids' favourite.

Second, Ridgebacks, or at least ridged dogs, were used as farm dogs over a much wider area than we would have expected, in the earlier parts of the 20th century. Therefore we must recognise as a fact that

'Natural guardian'. Sandra Carlson.

when Francis Richard Barnes gathered enthusiasts to discuss a standardisation of this genuine African dog, he merely selected a few examples of a phenomenon which was already established, and gave it the formal right of existence in the family of purebred dogs.

THE GENE POOL SPECTRUM

From the descriptions of the various colours and sizes of the reasonably recent ridged dogs which have been known, and combining this information with the broad geographic distribution at the time of formalising the breed, we must accept that the gene pool of our Ridgebacks of today shows great variation. Neither should we be shocked or even surprised if litters can still

Always alert and curious.

Photo: Rens Trappel, Netherlands.

produce rather dissimilar individuals.

Taking a single example: look at old pictures, and you find that many of the early 20th century dogs have half-erect ears. Even today ear positions can vary significantly, though modern breeding has managed to harmonise them to a great extent. We have also created the elegant, contemporary show ridge, a feature which, most certainly, is unlike the ridges which appeared on the backs of the early hunters and guard dogs. The original ridge formation was hair more or less standing up on the back. In addition, little, if anything, is known about the development of the two crowns, or the "arch", which is so prevalent today.

When Barnes took the decision to use the old Dalmatian Standard as a basis for the very first Ridgeback description he, consciously or unconsciously, made a firm decision that this should be a breed of classic hunting dog proportions. It is a dog that can move over long distances, and it hence has the rectangular, not square, body-proportions of a true hunter.

Whether the colour definition of light to red wheaten was a deliberate stroke of genius, or just a tribute to what looked African and what pleased the eye, is

The Ridgeback in action.

Photo: Radislav Viktorin, Czech Republic.

something else we will never know for sure. If, for instance, brindle – and why not dark-dark mahogany or Weimaraner silver – had been allowed, that would have given us a breed probably more true to the old hunting and farm dogs carrying ridges. However, the decision about colour was to be a fortunate one. By setting reasonably rigid standards for the coat colour, the founding fathers also helped in harmonising the gene pool. After all it must be considered highly likely that those ridged dogs that had conforming colours also had other similarities in common.

So, in the end, we have a 'Lion Dog' which in its colour is not far away either from the reddish African soil – or the lion itself.

RIDGEBACK TEMPERAMENT
Just as we have noted that knowledge about the early ridged dogs is more legend than fact, the true Ridgeback temperament is still much unknown territory. We will, in Chapter Six look at various studies, whereby we can start assessing breed-specific behaviour. Temperament testing of

dogs is in its infancy as a science. Interestingly, the canine behaviour experts that have left a real mark have been more exceptionally intelligent generalists than mathematical test supporters. (I recommend literature by Anders Hallgren, now active in the US, or Dr Abrantes in Denmark.)

The best descriptions of Ridgeback temperament still come from the experience of people who worked with the breed in the old days, combined with modern, skilled breeders. Tracking and hunting experience from places such as Canada has taught us about the versatility of the Ridgeback, which tracks both by air and ground contact. The vision of a Ridgeback is that of an alert big game hunter. The ability to cover, mentally, large areas has been well documented, not least in Sweden (Eva Bryntse, *Report to World Congress 1996* in Australia).

While for instance a German Shepherd finds it threatening to face three or more enemies approaching it in a forest, the Ridgeback keeps control over the entire field, and at a certain stage it makes its

The quality of being a safe guardsman, without any special guard training and without risking any action tougher than the situations demand, made the Ridgeback a popular farm dog in the latter part of the 19th century.

Picture courtesy:
H Tandefelt.

Ridgebacks love playing, action and chase. The best gift to a Ridgeback is a free-run – naturally under the control and supervision of his owner.

Photo: Katja Vogelsinger, Austria.

decision whether it will, as in the example from the story earlier in this chapter about the nightly walk, decide to move its master out of danger, or circle behind the approaching enemies with the aim of dispersing them.

We have proof of amazing hunting-related behaviour from people with lure coursing experience – though not all of it, by the way, gives high scores in lure coursing tests. For instance, the ability of a Ridgeback quickly to notice that the track is a closed circuit (US model) and that he can as easily wait for the lure to return, is not helpful! Some US examples show that Ridgebacks do not need specialisation, as we have dogs which have reached both show, tracking and obedience Championships. But it takes a skilled person to get all this out of a Ridgeback.

Classic assessment methods do not, by the way, always work so well on Ridgebacks. Many a 'temperament test' by working dog trainers has ended either in frustration or with really bad marks for Ridgebacks. As an example, we have the traditional test of 'action firmness', in which the dog shall swiftly attack the 'enemy's' padded arm. In some cases, the Ridgeback just rapidly backs off and starts circling the 'enemy', making sure it does not get hurt itself. In some documented cases the

Ridgebacks play "rough, tough but fair". A pair of Ridgebacks can play for amazingly long periods of time. Much of the play is "wrestling", with the dogs keep close contact. This natural training for real fights – which Ridgebacks very seldom enage in – is interrupted by irresistible urges to run.

Picture courtesy: H Tandefelt.

lightning-quick avoidance tactic has been followed by an attack against an unpadded part of the body – and, as a great example of the Ridgeback's self-control, the bites have been painful, but yet have been more warning signals than bites out of aggression.

TRUE RIDGEBACK PRIDE

If I were to highlight a single quality in the Ridgeback, it is pride. This is a self-assured dog, which knows its own speed, its own agility and its own competence. The dark eyes of a Ridgeback gleam with interest as soon as something new happens. But never treat a Ridgeback badly. Even though we should avoid giving dogs human characteristics, I can guarantee that the Ridgeback has a long memory. Well-treated, he is always your most devoted companion. All he asks for is to be shown the same loyalty, plus a genuine respect for his integrity. Sometimes, when you think that the independent arrogance in your Ridgeback is going a step too far, remember that he is a proud dog, and has a lot to be proud about.

PERFECT BALANCE

The ground we have covered so far in fact points to amazing extremes – the swiftness in the movements, making the Ridgeback able to avoid fast-moving dangers; the almost uninterested slowness when nothing exciting is happening; the power needed in a farm dog to fend off both human and animal intruders; the lightness in movements, mile after mile after mile. No horse-riding tour is too long for a Ridgeback to follow with ease. Then there is the fierce courage when the dog's master is threatened combined with the soft devotion to his friends and especially to children.

There is, in fact, a single way of describing this combination of remarkable power, swift movement, endurance and explosive alertness: it is *balance*. Or, if we

The pride of the Ridgeback stems from a dog that is completely confident of his own powers.

The Ridgeback is not the fastest of breeds, but shows amazing speed in combination with endurance and agility. *Photo: Courtesy of Studio Roberto, Germany.*

want to put it in a more memorable way, *the only extreme feature in a Ridgeback is an absolute lack of extremes.*

The general impression of a Ridgeback is one of elegance, combined with a sense of power. It means, in judging terms, that if the absolute balance is not there when you take a few steps back and view the dog, it is not the ideal Ridgeback. There is no doubt that the male, in its masculinity, is a bit more powerful than the bitch, with every inch communicating swiftness and speed. Still, the male should never be powerful to the point where more power than speed becomes evident. And, correspondingly, while admiring the elegance of the Ridgeback bitch, you should never condone a lack of muscle in favour of femininity.

It is noteworthy that, for instance in Australia, where the lure coursing tracks are shorter and demand high sideways mobility, Ridgebacks have been competing at the very top. It is equally interesting to discover how much Ridgebacks love one of those canine sports of the future, Agility. This is said with the caveat that the Ridgeback, in its enthusiasm for anything that is full of fun and action, might decide, absolutely on its own, that a few of the obstacles are really great and just rush through them twice.

The herding instincts also exist in a Ridgeback, but not at all to the same extent as the hunting and guarding capabilities. This does not always stop a slightly insufficiently trained Ridgeback bringing a deer, or another larger animal, to you. Fortunately Ridgebacks seldom attack and harm larger animals unless trained to do so, though small prey such as hares sometimes form irresistible hunting objects, especially for bitches. The Ridgeback world is aware of the fact that Ridgebacks have been used in small teams of three to four dogs, to hunt down and kill wild boars. I find this neither very tasteful nor wise, though it does add one more aspect to the description of the multi-faceted talents of a Ridgeback.

OWNER CONTROL
With this versatility in mind, I dare to say that any real dog owner, or any good dog owner who wants a real dog, will find

*The high grass is home for a Ridgeback, be it
on the African fields or European or
American slopes.
Photo: M. Ygre, Norway.*

ample opportunities to enjoy such companionship with a Ridgeback. At the same time, I cannot repeat often enough that possessing such a fast, strong, alert dog requires complete control by the owner. Our breed is just far too good to be given a bad name just because the owner might not understand the true nature of this dog. The Ridgeback is a natural dog, and it must be treated as such. This is neither a lap dog, nor a pet for people who shun exercise and nature, and possibly even not a first dog for beginners. The Ridgeback is an ideal dog for people who have come to appreciate the full range of abilities – and the capacity for companionship – possessed by a dog with strong links back to wild, untamed nature.

The Ridgeback owner must command full control of his dog. This is not achieved by aggressive demands. The only way to control a Ridgeback fully is to earn his or her full respect.

3 *EVALUATING A RIDGEBACK*

The Ridgeback became what it is, an individual breed, mainly because its qualities were noticed thanks to the unique hair formation on the dog's back (see Chapter One). The Ridge is, as we will see when discussing shows and show potential, one of the key features of the breed. However, we must also remember that what really makes today's Ridgeback such a wonderful companion is what is below the Ridge. In today's world, a century after the breed became seriously noticed, more and more veterinary experts question the morality of culling Ridgeless puppies just because they have no Ridge, when they are completely healthy animals. With radical hindsight it could be said that, in the period 1922-24, the decision could have been taken to have a Ridged 'real Ridgeback', and an African Hunting Dog, with identical qualities but no Ridge – and possibly also with other colours allowed. This did not happen, and though it might still become a reality in the 21st century, what we need to do today is evaluate the breed called Rhodesian Ridgeback among the some 300 pure-breed dog types that we have.

In the first years of the Ridgeback it was classified as a Gun Dog – not entirely incorrectly, though that classification tended to distract from the dog's parallel quality, that of a natural and even-tempered guardian. In the British terminology we today talk about a breed in the Hound group. A somewhat difficult concept, as it includes all kinds of dogs such as Dachshunds, Elk Hounds (spitz type dogs), the Basset Hounds, Bloodhounds, Coonhounds etc. It means that in show terms Ridgebacks compete with Basenjis, Beagles, Afghan Hounds, Greyhounds, Whippets and Foxhounds. This is a highly mixed bag. The FCI Group 6 is a bit more even, though many of the contrasts are still there. Ridgebacks are, in the group finals, measured against Otterhounds as well as Beagles, Bassets and Bloodhounds, but also a large number of similarly built hunting-type dogs. It is known that the founding fathers of Ridgebacks, the men around Mr Barnes, took the old Dalmatian Standard as a guide when formulating the first Ridgeback Standard. Still today we find breeds which show similar proportions, and

The first impression of a Ridgeback must be that of an upstanding, rectangular dog, conveying strength and elegance, with a keen, alert expression. Photo: M. Bernkopf, Austria.

heads, to the Ridgeback; Dalmatians, Weimaraners, Vizslas, and even the longhaired Berger de Bries have bodies that are not far from the Ridgeback outlines. What this chapter tries to achieve is to tell the reader how the Ridgeback is composed.

MAKING THE STANDARDS COME ALIVE

THE FIRST IMPRESSION

The dog in front of you is of upper medium size, upstanding and proud, showing alertness and possibly an arrogant lack of interest in you. His body is markedly longer than his height, the angulation is balanced and sufficient for a long-distance runner, the chest is deep and the front is strong enough to be seen from the side. The dog is also in good physical condition.

Good – this is the first impression you want from a Rhodesian Ridgeback.

In addition, should there be long, lean muscles, firm feet and strong though never heavy bone, this individual can be considered of great value. You just need to make sure the ridge is long enough, is symmetrical and has two, and only two,

The Ridgeback is a upper medium-sized breed. The body is rectangular, never square-shaped. The body-length enables the dog to move with long, sound strides.

Photo: Veronica Gomes-Hansson, Sweden.

crowns. Pending proof of a balanced temperament, you are looking at a potential winner. The total balance you have seen signals a correct Ridgeback, long before starting to check the dog in detail. You might then still be disappointed, because the single most important feature of this working breed is perfect movement; but the likelihood is that a dog that fits the foregoing description will also show correct movement.

When you take that first look (taking one step back to make sure you really are focused on the whole entity), remember the criterion that the only extreme is a total lack of extremes.

THE HEAD
The Ridgeback head is both classically simple, yet full of expression. Being very much a 'basic dog', expect identical proportions in the head: that is that the skull is equal in length and width (in an adult dog), and the length of the muzzle is identical with that of the skull. The stop should be reasonably well-defined, and the top lines of the skull and the muzzle must be uncompromisingly parallel. A Ridgeback head must never give a triangular impression, viewed either from the front or the side.

The muzzle of a Ridgeback is strong and deep, with a full and correct scissor bite. The head should have a certain 'sharpness', with ears carried close to the head and starting from the upper skull line when the dog is alert. Lips should fit closely.

The eyes should be reasonably well-rounded, set well apart and express alertness. An individual with a dark nose should have dark eyes; a liver-nosed dog must have amber eyes (not colourless, sometimes bluish eyes). Watch out for strong sunshine when evaluating dogs, as this might cause a wrong impression of eye colour to be given.

Black on muzzle and ears is correct, though a one-coloured muzzle is equal in value in the show ring.

The Ridgeback is a breed that shows a marked distinction between males and females, and one should expect masculinity and femininity, within the above parameters, to be easily distinctive in any individual.

NECK AND FRONT
The neck should be long enough to give an elegant balance. It should be strongly muscled, never coarse, and free of throatiness.

The front (prosternum) is most essential for the muscular length of the body, and hence endurance. A good Ridgeback has a prosternum that can be seen from the side

The head is masculine in a male, with the proportions of skull width equalling muzzle length, and with a well-defined stop.
Photo: Marlo Boeffel, UK.

The toplines of the skull and the upper side of the muzzle shall be fully parallel in a good Ridgeback head. Any deviation from this parallelity is a fault.
Photo: Katja Vogelsinger. Austria.

The female head should be distinctly feminine, yet with adequate strength and with a powerful muzzle.
Photo: Susan Clayborough.

The stop needs to be well-defined, still retaining the correct proportions of the head.
Photo: AnnMarie Hilding.

The young Ridgeback should not show a skull width that is too marked before an age of 10 to 16 months. This five-month male puppy shows excellent promise.
Photo: AnneMarie Hilding, Sweden.

The eyes should be alert and interested. A Ridgeback that fails to give an impression of alertness in the show ring should not get top marks.
Photo: Rens Trappel, Netherlands.

The ears start in line with the skull and lie close to the head when the dog is alert. The eyes are dark in a dark-nosed dog. A top-class head is balanced, without coarseness or any shade of heaviness.
Photo: S. Marek, Germany.

The brown or liver-nosed Ridgeback should have lighter eyes, yet with a warm pigmentation in the eye. A 'light amber' eye is a good description.
Photo: Bruno Hachet, France.

The neck should be long and elegant, the front strong with a visible pro sternum when viewed from the side, and the angulation should be balanced and equal in front and rear. Note how well the chest reaches to the elbow in this outstanding bitch.

Photo: Courtesy of the RR Club of New South Wales.

of the dog, and easily noted when placing a hand across the front of the dog. Weak fronts are a major functional fault.

BODY AND CHEST

The body proportions should be 5:4 length to height, or a shade more for females.

The chest should be deep and capacious and the front strong, but never too broad ('barrel chest') to hamper the swift side movements of a Ridgeback. The perfect chestline curves upwards elegantly towards the rear of the dog. Photo: Carina Pergren, Sweden.

Short-bodied Ridgebacks are not functional.

The chest should be capacious and deep, with the lower chest-line, in an adult Ridgeback, reaching the knee level. The ribcage should be long, ideally ending in an elegant curve towards the short loin.

Seen from the front, the chest shall be of sufficient strength but never too broad, which would severely hamper the breed-typical side movements. The chest shall be formed by elegantly curved ribs, never a broad 'barrel-chest'.

LEGS AND FEET

The legs shall have bones in balance with the overall size and composition of the dog. The bones must not be too weak for the muscle power, but never heavy or rounded, limiting the impression of swiftness and speed.

The feet shall be sufficiently high, with well-arched toes to secure endurance, assuming toes long and strong enough to make the dog a good climber.

Pads should be strong, protected with hair between the toes and pads.

SHOULDERS

The angulation of shoulders and rear legs

must be in perfect balance to allow optimal length of ground-covering stride. The shoulders should be well laid back and elbows kept close to the body.

MUSCLES
Being a long-distance runner, the Ridgeback should have well-developed as well as properly trained, long and lean muscles (not short, 'boxer-type' muscles).

TAIL AND CROUP
Ideally reaching the hocks, the tail should be strong, elegantly tapering towards the end and free of coarseness. The tail-set should be neither too low, with tail root pointing downwards, denoting a curved croup, nor directly in line with the topline of the body. A tail-root pointing upwards denotes a steep croup. At a fast trot the tail root (first 10-15 cms) should be kept parallel with the ground, signalling a balanced croup construction.

COLOURS
The Ridgeback should be light to red wheaten, assuming that all these colours show a tone of warmth. Too light ('light fawn') colours lacking warm nuances, or dark mahogany, past a red nuance in the colour, are equally incorrect.

The dog can have black on the muzzle and ears, with some dark hair on the tip of the tail permissible. White on toes and, within reasonable limits, in front is considered correct. Excessive white, as well as black in the coat outside muzzle and ears, must be judged as incorrect.

In the show ring, all shades of colour within the Standard should be treated as equal in quality.

The coat shall be short and soundly dense, with a shine, though never woolly or silky. The correct coat is also protective, not cosmetic.

THE RIDGE
The ridge is the original escutcheon of the breed, now refined by man into near perfection. The ridge, the hair growing in the opposite direction to the rest of the coat, shall start immediately behind the shoulders and taper towards the end, which shall reach at least the front side of the upper thighs. In order to merit the comment "excellent ridge", the dog should have a perfectly symmetrical ridge, the arch 'box' included, and it should reach the mid part of the thighs. The upper end should start with an arch, under which two 'crowns' (whorls) are symmetrically placed on each side of the ridge. The ideal width of the ridge, in relation to the dog's size, is approximately 2.5 ins (5 cms) just behind the arch. The proportion of the arch down to the crowns, measured as part of the entire ridge, should not exceed one third of the total ridge length.

A Ridgeback with fewer or more than two crowns, or distinctly too short a ridge, shall be deemed incompatible with the breed requirements and cannot be given an award at a dog show.

SIZE
The height of a Ridgeback male is set between 63 to 69 cms (25 to 27 inches); the Ridgeback female should be between 61 and 66 cms (24 to 26 inches), measured from the withers and assuming the dog stands straight on its front feet.

(The weight indication, which incorrectly

RIDGEBACK COLOURS

Light wheaten – the warm nuance is not dominant but still discernible.
Photo: Susan Clayborough, Norway.

Maturing light wheaten. In colder climates the Ridgeback develops a tighter, thicker undercoat. This gives the coat a somewhat lighter shine.
Photo: Per Nygaard, Norway.

Warm medium wheaten. A common colour in English and Nordic Ridgebacks.

Mature medium wheaten – the warmth of the colour shows a slight tone of red. Possibly the most common colour in a Ridgeback.
Photo: Birgitta Ebkar, Sweden.

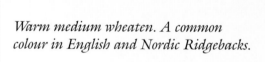

RIDGEBACK COLOURS

Medium red wheaten. A balance between brown wheaten and reddish nuances gives a gleam of sunset warmth to the colour of the dog.
Photo: M. Yrge, Norway.

Mature red wheaten. The warmth shines through to a maximum – the most spectacular colour of a Ridgeback.
Photo: Crawford-Manton, Ireland.

Dark red wheaten, the darkest the Ridgeback colour gets before the warm nuances fade away and are replaced by colours that can be described as 'dark brown' or 'dark mahogany'.

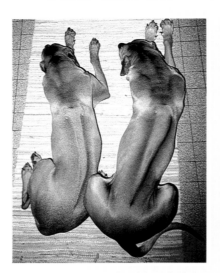

The Ridge is symmetric, evenly tapering towards the tip. This means the ridge must be of sufficient width at the upper end (towards the arch and crown). Photo: Helen Engfelt, Sweden.

The arch, previously also called the 'box', encompasses the two symmetrically placed hair whorls – the crowns. The arch can cover a maximum of one-third the total length of the ridge (including the arch). The Standard allows several shapes for the arch, all to be treated equally. However, the arch should be symmetrical.

The ridge is, together with the overall balance and the movement, the most significant feature of a Ridgeback. The ridge must therefore be correct in symmetry and length, with the correct number and placement of the crowns. Any number, other than two crowns, is directly disqualifying.

While it is imperative that the ridge has only two crowns, symmetrically opposite each other, it is also of major importance that the ridge is of sufficient length. Ridges that are too short must be judged as faulty. Photo: Courtesy of the RR Club of Queensland.

does not take into account any variation between dogs of various heights, is impractical and hence of no value when evaluating a dog.)

MOVEMENT

Movement is essential in any breed and of exceptional importance in a mobile, natural dog such as a Ridgeback. The efficiency of motion should be measured in the actual ground coverage (on an even surface). The front and rear feet should cover identical amounts of ground.

The Ridgeback gait must be low and effective, avoiding high front movement (for instance the 'hackney gait') and high hind-leg kick-ups losing ground contact before the paws have reached their hindmost position.

Seen from the front, the dog shall move with parallel front movement, though a dog standing still can have a slight outward bend in the front feet.

Seen from the rear, the feet should move close to each other at a fast trot, with hind legs which are neither bent out ('bow-hocked') nor tight in hocks ('cow-hocked'). Note that close hind quarters can never be evaluated when the dog is standing still.

A Ridgeback in good physical condition shall move with elegant ease and lightness, which is especially visible in the slow trot.

TEMPERAMENT

An adult Ridgeback shows neither shyness nor fear when approached by a stranger. It is allowed to be arrogantly aloof, but never aggressive. It is essential to expect that a Ridgeback in the show ring communicates alertness and curiosity about the environment.

THE FCI STANDARD

ORIGIN South Africa.
Standard supplied by the Kennel Union of Southern Africa and the Zimbabwe Kennel Club.
Date of publication of the valid original standard 10.12.1995

UTILIZATION The Rhodesian Ridgeback is still used to hunt game in many parts of the world, but is especially prized as watch-dog and family pet.

FCI CLASSIFICATION Group 6: Scent hounds and related breeds.
Section 3 Related breeds.
Without working trial.

BRIEF HISTORICAL SUMMARY The Rhodesian Ridgeback is presently the only registered breed indigenous to southern Africa. Its forbears can be traced to the Cape Colony of southern Africa, where they crossed with the early pioneers' dogs and the semi-domesticated, ridged Hottentot hunting dogs. Hunting mainly in groups of two or three, the original function of the Rhodesian Ridgeback or Lion dog was to track game, especially lion, and, with great agility, keep it at bay until the arrival of the hunter.
The original standard, which was drafted by F.R. Barnes, in Bulawayo, Rhodesia, in 1922, was based on that of the Dalmatian and was approved by the South African Kennel Union in 1926.

GENERAL APPEARANCE The Rhodesian Ridgeback should represent a well balanced, strong, muscular, agile and

The movement of a Ridgeback in trot is light, almost dancing. The ideal Ridgeback has long, well-trained muscles. Short and rounded muscles do not produce endurance over long distances. Note the correct set of the tail-root in motion, denoting a perfect croup.

A sound-moving Ridgeback gaits with his (or her) head slightly up when in slow motion. In fast trot, the neckline is lowered to the level of the topline of the dog. Note the excellent, low movements of this Ridgeback. Any upward movement in the front legs is a major hindrance to efficiency and must be penalised in the show ring.
Photo: Mariette de Veer, Netherlands.

The Ridgeback is never shown at full speed in a show ring. It is, however, essential that a Ridgeback owner and breeder understands all the paces.
Photo: M. Bernkopf, Austria.

The Ridgeback is a proud, alert dog, which must show neither nervousness nor fear when approached by strangers.

active dog, symmetrical in outline, and capable of great endurance with a fair amount of speed. The emphasis is on agility, elegance and soundness with no tendency towards massiveness. The peculiarity of the breed is the ridge on the back, which is formed by the hair growing in the opposite direction to the rest of the coat. The ridge is the escutcheon of the breed. The ridge must be clearly defined, symmetrical and tapering towards the haunch. It must start immediately behind the shoulders and continue to the hip (haunches) bones. The ridge must contain only two crowns, identical and opposite each other. The lower edges of the crowns must not extend further down the ridge than one-third of its length. A good average width of the ridge is 5 cm (2 ins).

BEHAVIOUR/TEMPERAMENT
Dignified, intelligent, aloof with strangers, but showing no aggression or shyness.

HEAD
CRANIAL REGION Skull: Should be of a fair length (width of head between ears, distance from occiput to stop, stop to end of nose, should be equal), flat and broad between the ears; the head should be free from wrinkles when in repose.

Stop: The stop should be reasonably well defined and not in one straight line from the nose to the occipital bone.

FACIAL REGION
Nose: The nose should be black or brown. A black nose should be accompanied by dark eyes, a brown nose by amber eyes.

Muzzle: The muzzle should be long, deep and powerful.

Lips: The lips should be clean, closely fitting the jaws.

Mouth: Jaws strong, with a perfect and complete scissor bite, i.e. the upper teeth closely overlapping the lower teeth and set square to the jaws. The teeth must be well developed, especially the canines or holders.

Cheeks: Cheeks should be clean.

Eyes: Should be moderately well apart, round, bright and sparkling, with intelligent expression, their colour harmonising with the colour of the coat.

Ears: Should be set rather high, of

medium size, rather wide at base, and gradually tapering to a rounded point. They should be carried close to the head.

NECK: Should be fairly long, strong and free from throatiness.

BODY
Back: Powerful.
Loins: Strong, muscular and slightly arched.
Chest: Should not be too wide, but very deep and capacious; the brisket should reach to the elbow.
Forechest: Should be visible when viewed from the side.
Ribs: Moderately well sprung, never rounded like barrel-hoops.

TAIL: Should be strong at the root and gradually tapering towards the end, free from coarseness. It should be of moderate length. It should not be attached too high nor too low, and should be carried with a slight curve upwards, never curled.

FOREQUARTERS: The forelegs should be perfectly straight, strong and well boned, with the elbows close to the body. When viewed from the side, the forelegs should be wider than viewed from the front. Pasterns should be strong with slight spring.
Shoulders: The shoulders should be sloping, clean and muscular, denoting speed.
Feet: The feet should be compact and round, with well arched toes; and tough elastic pads, protected by hair between the toes and pads.

HINDQUARTERS: In the hind legs the muscles should be clean, well defined, good turn of stifle and strong hocks well let down.
GAIT/MOVEMENT: Straight forward, free and active.

COAT
HAIR: Should be short and dense, sleek and glossing in appearance, but neither woolly nor silky.
COLOUR: Light wheaten to red wheaten. A little white on the chest and toes is permissible, but excessive white hairs here, on belly, or above toes is undesirable. A dark muzzle and ears permissible. Excessive black hairs throughout the coat are highly undesirable.

SIZE
The desirable heights are:

Dogs:	63 cm (25 ins) to
	69 cm (27 ins).
Bitches:	61 cm (24 ins) to
	66 cm (26 ins).

WEIGHT
The desirable weights are:

| Dogs | 36.5 kg (80 lbs) |
| Bitches | 32 kg (70 lbs). |

FAULTS: Any departure from the foregoing points should be considered a fault and the seriousness with which the fault should be regarded should be in exact proportion to its degree.

N.B.: Male animals should have two apparently normal testicles fully descended into the scrotum.

THE BRITISH STANDARD

GENERAL APPEARANCE Handsome, strong, muscular and active dog, symmetrical in outline, capable of great endurance with fair amount of speed. Mature dog is handsome and upstanding.

CHARACTERISTICS Peculiarity is the ridge on back formed by hair growing in opposite direction to the remainder of coat; ridge must be regarded as the escutcheon of the breed. Ridge clearly defined, tapering and symmetrical, starting immediately behind shoulders and continuing to haunch, and containing two identical crowns only, opposite each other, lower edges of crowns not extending further down ridge than one-third of its length. Up to 5 cm (2 in) is a good average for width of ridge.

TEMPERAMENT Dignified, intelligent, aloof with strangers but showing no aggression or shyness.

HEAD AND SKULL Of fair length, skull flat, rather broad between ears, free from wrinkles when in repose. Stop reasonably well defined.

NOSE Black or brown in keeping with colour of dog. Black nose accompanied by dark eyes, brown nose by amber eyes. Muzzle long, deep and powerful. Lips clean and close fitting.

EYES Set moderately well apart, round, bright and sparkling with intelligent expression, colour harmonising with coat colour.

EARS Set rather high, medium size, rather wide at base, gradually tapering to a rounded point. Carried close to head.

MOUTH Jaws strong, with a perfect, regular and complete scissor bite, i.e. upper teeth closely overlapping lower teeth and set square to the jaws. Well developed teeth, especially canines.

NECK Fairly long, strong and free from throatiness.

FOREQUARTERS Shoulders sloping, clean and muscular. Forelegs perfectly straight, strong, heavy in bone; elbows close to body.

BODY Chest not too wide, very deep and capacious; ribs moderately well sprung, never barrel-ribbed. Back powerful; loins strong, muscular and slightly arched.

HINDQUARTERS Muscles clean, well defined; good turn of stifle; hocks well let down.

FEET Compact, well arched toes; round, tough, elastic pads, protected by hair between toes and pads.

TAIL Strong at root, not inserted high or low, tapering towards end, free from coarseness. Carried with a slight curve upwards, never curled.

GAIT/MOVEMENT Straight forward, free and active.

COAT Short and dense, sleek and glossy in appearance but neither woolly nor silky.

COLOUR Light wheaten to red wheaten. Head, body, legs and tail of uniform colour. Little white on chest and toes permissible, but excessive white hairs here, on belly or above paws undesirable. Dark muzzle and ears permissible.
SIZE Dogs: 63 cm (25 in) desirable minimum height at withers; 67 (27 in) desirable maximum height at withers; bitches: 61 cm (24 in) desirable minimum height at withers; 66 cm (26 in) desirable maximum height at withers.*

FAULTS Any departure from the foregoing points should be considered a fault and the seriousness with which the fault should be regarded should be in exact proportion to its degree.

NOTE Male animals should have two apparently normal testicles fully descended into the scrotum.

Reproduced by kind permission of the Kennel Club.

*NOTE: The centimetre figure is an incorrect translation of 27 ins, which is a correct figure.

THE AMERICAN STANDARD
Approved August 11th, 1992

GENERAL APPEARANCE The Ridgeback represents a strong, muscular and active dog, symmetrical and balanced in outline. A mature Ridgeback is a handsome, upstanding and athletic dog, capable of great endurance with a fair (good) amount of speed. Of even, dignified temperament, the Ridgeback is devoted and affectionate to his master, reserved with strangers. The peculiarity of the breed is the *ridge* on the back. The ridge must be regarded as the characteristic feature of the breed.

SIZE, PROPORTION, SUBSTANCE A mature Ridgeback should be symmetrical in outline, slightly longer than tall but well balanced. Dogs: 25 to 27 inches in height; Bitches: 24 to 26 inches in height. Desirable weight: Dogs: 85 pounds; Bitches: 70 pounds.

HEAD Should be of fair length, the skull flat and rather broad between the ears and should be free from wrinkles when in repose. The stop should be reasonably well defined. EYES Should be moderately well apart, and should be round, bright and sparkling, with intelligent expression, their color harmonizing with the color of the dog. EARS Should be set rather high, of medium size, rather wide at base, and tapering to a rounded point. They should be carried close to the head. MUZZLE Should be long, deep and powerful. The lips clean, closely fitting the jaws. NOSE Should be black, or brown, in keeping with the color of the dog. No other colored nose is permissible.
   A black nose should be accompanied by dark eyes, a brown or liver nose with amber eyes.

NECK, TOPLINE, BODY The neck should be fairly strong and free from throatiness. The chest should not be too wide, but very deep and capacious, ribs moderately well sprung, never rounded like barrel hoops (which would indicate want of speed). The back is powerful and firm with strong loins which are muscular and slightly arched. The tail should be strong at the insertion and generally tapering towards the end, free from coarseness. It should not be inserted too high or too low and should be carried with a slight curve upwards, never curled or gay.

FOREQUARTERS The shoulders should be sloping, clean and muscular, denoting speed. Elbows close to the body. The forelegs should be perfectly straight, strong and heavy in bone. The feet should be compact with well-arched toes, round, tough, elastic pads, protected by hair between the toes and pads. Dewclaws may be removed.

HINDQUARTERS In the hind legs the muscles should be clean, well defined and hocks well down. Feet as in front.

COAT Should be short and dense, sleek and glossy in appearance, but neither woolly nor silky.

COLOUR Light wheaten to red wheaten. A little white on the chest and toes permissible but excessive white there, on the belly or above the toes is undesirable.

RIDGE The hall mark of this breed is the *ridge* on the back which is formed by the hair growing in the opposite direction to the rest of the coat. The ridge must be regarded as the characteristic feature of the breed. The ridge should be clearly defined, tapering and symmetrical. It should start immediately behind the shoulders and continue to a point between the prominence of the hips and should contain two identical crowns (whorls) directly opposite each other. The lower edge of the crowns (whorls) should not extend further down the ridge than one third of the ridge.

Disqualification: Ridgelessness. Serious Fault: One crown (whorl) or more than two crowns (whorls).

GAIT At the trot, the back is held level and the stride is efficient, long, free and unrestricted. Reach and drive expressing a perfect balance between power and elegance. At the chase, the Ridgeback demonstrates great coursing ability and endurance.

TEMPERAMENT Dignified and even tempered. Reserved with strangers.

SCALE OF POINTS

General appearance, size, symmetry and balance	20
Ridge	20
Head	15
Legs and feet	15
Neck and shoulders	10
Body, back, chest and loin	10
Coat and color	5
Tail	5
Total	100

Reproduced by kind permission of the American Kennel Club.

4 DECIDING ON A RIDGEBACK

If you have read this far then we can assume that you are either a dog owner or are planning to buy a dog. Whether or not to own a dog is a decision to ponder long and hard and with complete family involvement. Dog ownership in real life is always different from dog ownership in theory.

THE COMMITMENT

Ownership requires more work, more willingness also to adapt to the dog's requirements, than we expect. There might be a sudden event created by work, or a potential pleasure activity, that can be hampered by having a dog. The early Sunday morning walk in bad weather is not always fun, at least for the first few minutes. But you cannot compromise with the need for walks.

Dog ownership is not ownership in the way we normally use the word: it is companionship. You give and you take. In the end, you get a lot more back than you ever put in. This loyal devotion, friendship and willingness to serve has made the canine family unique in the evolution of the

animal kingdom – and in this I include that most unpredictable inhabitant, homo sapiens.

The basic decision about adding a dog to your family must also take into account your career plan, both the part you can

Think carefully before taking on the commitment of owning a Ridgeback.

Photo: Tonje Torkelsen, Norway.

organise, and the part you cannot, which is called promotion. Not all countries are as hospitable as the ones that are, for instance, included in this book. During my professional career I have had to say that some countries were off-limits because of my interest in dogs and my ownership of dogs. This has not always been entirely popular or in line with corporate policy – which, in many cases, is another name for avoiding flexibility or not having much of a human touch!

RIDGEBACK OWNERSHIP

Here are the main points which anyone who considers owning, or who already owns a young Ridgeback, should be aware of. I describe each point in more detail throughout this chapter.

The Ridgeback is a natural, mobile dog. It assumes that its owner is willing to take the time needed, every day and in every weather, to give it sufficient exercise. If your reaction is "so this is not a very suitable city dog", you are correct. There are always exceptions, with exceptional dog owners, but a Ridgeback is the son or daughter of the open fields.

The Ridgeback is multi-talented and versatile. This also means it is not likely to be an absolute top winner in sports that demand a high degree of specialisation. Lure-coursing seems to be one of those interesting exceptions. On the other hand, your dog loves every activity you offer him, and the more you do it as a team, the more he will love every day of his life.

The attention span of a Ridgeback is rather short. Another way of saying it is that the genuine curiosity of a Ridgeback goes with a certain lack of patience. This means that any training must be done in short intervals, that training a Ridgeback must mean a lot of fun, and also that mixing training themes is an advantage.

Avoid training – or temperament-testing – methods that are developed, for instance, for traditional police dogs or other working breeds. The Ridgeback's behaviour is different from these breeds and the end result is normally, at least, a frustrated trainer, a dissapointed owner, and in the worst-case scenario a confused and frustrated Ridgeback.

A Ridgeback is a natural, balanced guard dog. It does not require any training for this, particularly training which could lead to the introduction of aggressive tendencies. These do not come naturally and can result in anti-social behaviour.

Ridgebacks are patient and good with children. This means that it is your responsibility to make sure the children are equally good with the dog. If you choose to raise a family which includes a dog, this dog must have its natural rights.

Being a natural dog and also a strong, agile one, a Ridgeback must never, ever be involved in fights with other dogs. Just as with human beings, situations involving conflict can occur, and it is the owner's absolute responsibility to train the Ridgeback to obey commands when challenged by other dogs.

In the show ring, an alert, correct Ridgeback must still behave properly. Too many times in too many countries have Ridgebacks been seen as 'trouble makers' in the show ring. This is bad ring handling and has nothing to do with an 'aggressive temperament'. Producing Ridgebacks that have no 'go' left in them, and which are

standing asleep in the show ring, is not the answer. On the contrary, that is the last thing we would like to see our breed develop into. The challenge is to produce a natural, sound Ridgeback and a skilled owner, capable of performing good handling tactics in the ring as a team.

One of the many wonderful sides to a Ridgeback is that it is a healthy breed that has the potential to be an active companion well into its later years. Do not stop the exercise when your Ridgeback becomes a veteran, but go on giving him his required time outdoors. He remains playful and positive to the very end of his life, which, when we talk about our canine friends, is always so unfairly short.

THE RIGHT BREED?
The decision is made. You want a dog. Have you had any experience with dogs previously, either you or your husband or

Experience in dog ownership is required when dealing with the challenge a Ridgeback presents. Photo: Michael Bernkopf, Austria.

wife or partner? If not, think once more before you consider owning a Ridgeback. It can work out well, but really the Ridgeback is not suitable to be a first dog. A Ridgeback is very large and demanding; this is a very natural animal which offers little in the way of compromise. It is not a Golden Retriever type, a gentle dog that does anything to accommodate your smallest wish. The Ridgeback requires large quantities of physical and mental stimulation. Do not misunderstand me. I know that the Golden Retriever, and indeed all breeds, deserve respect and stimulation, but they need it in other ways. Even a rather big breed, such as a Labrador or a Golden Retriever, is, at the age of eight to ten weeks, still a soft, cuddly baby. A two-month-old Ridgeback is a high-energy package who asks for more from week to week.

And the question has to be asked, where and how do you live? The ideal for a Ridgeback is a house with a fenced-in garden. This does not mean that you can avoid the long walks and, hopefully, one day the biking tours. It just makes your early Ridgeback life easier for you. Living in the middle of a city with a Ridgeback should not really be considered. If you are thinking about taking this course of action, think twice more.

MALE OR FEMALE?
The question of whether a male or a female dog is easier to handle is one of the eternal – and usually friendly – debates. There is also no proof that your choice should be affected by whether the dog is to be predominantly male, or predominantly female, owned. There is an old saying that a

Rain, wind or snow – the Ridgeback is always ready for a walk.
Photo: Michael Bernkopf, Austria.

lady is too weak to handle a big male. As far as dogs are concerned, we assume that the lady who is planning to buy a Ridgeback also intends to have good contact with the dog and to teach the dog basic discipline. A Ridgeback is never a dog you send your six-year-old child out to walk. But a Ridgeback, like any normal, sound breed, should be trained properly, for the sake of your safety and that of the dog.

The Ridgeback has it roots firmly in nature, and therefore there is a marked difference in the average mental composition of males and females. The male is more steady – if this word can ever be used with a Ridgeback. These dogs are reliable, yes; but steady, in the sense of never wanting to play, or have a little extra run or a bit of mischief, no. He can be noisy with other males, but this is not an overly aggressive breed. He is definitely more of a guardsman, with excellent hunting qualities. It is the female who is the outstanding hunter with excellent guarding qualities. The male will be more likely to go overboard in showing sheer, uncomplicated devotion. The female always has that little extra twinkle in her eyes, and there is frequently in her a readiness for that little extra fun. Sometimes you like it, sometimes not!

THE BREEDING FACTOR

In addition to considerations about differences in behaviour there is the simple question of being interested in breeding, or not. This is another of those questions which, like dog ownership and choice of breed, should not be taken lightly. If your answer is another yes, then add a lot of time and work to the search for your first Ridgeback female.

Even if you buy your dog as a pet, you must prepare yourself to test out the various breeders, to ask relevant questions about the soundness of their dogs, to meet the breeders themselves, and to inspect the parents of your potential puppy.

If you intend to start breeding, it is even more important to find out about the hereditary qualities of your dog. For example, if you decide that you will not breed from your bitch, you could agree to accept a nice puppy from a litter where ridgeless puppies have been born and in which, on average, only one quarter of the litter carry a dominant quality for a ridge. The statistical probability of your puppy being twice as likely to be heterozygous for ridge than of being homozygous does not matter at all. The mental qualities, the physical aspects, are all the same and you can have a long and happy relationship with your dog.

But if you do want to breed, read the section about Ridge genetics a few extra times, and choose a bitch from parents which have been tested in different combinations, and where you have reliable data about litters from all the grandparents

If you are planning to breed from your Ridgeback, there are many important criteria to consider.

as well. This works pretty well in most of the more developed Ridgeback countries. Sometimes there will, no doubt, be a little more guesswork. But you still need to ask all those questions.

By the way, the above advice also goes for buyers of male dogs. Only if you know for sure that your pet male will never be used at stud should you, for instance, not worry too much about the hereditary qualities for ridge. You might even offer a home to a ridgeless puppy.

However, it could be that you, as the person who would never, ever breed and never show, find that you, or your daughter or son becomes really interested in dogs and in dog competitions. So what then about buying a ridgeless puppy? I am going to stick my neck out and say that, if the temperament is fine and the breeders match your quality demands, go ahead. You will have saved a young life and you will get full enjoyment out of the dog and so will your daughter or son. Your Ridgeback-minus-ridge will just love the Lure Coursing, Agility, Tracking, Flyball, or whatever it is that you do. In addition, the interesting experience you and your family gathers, be it in the shape of, for instance, obedience or test results, or just cute anecdotes, will provide valuable information about our breed and its mental composition. A ridgeless Ridgeback is a Ridgeback without a ridge, but it lacks nothing else.

BUYING A "SHOW DOG"
I am sorry to disappoint you, but there is no such thing as buying a "show dog". All you can do is to make sure that there are no exterior faults, such as incorrect colours, or a lack of ridge, or a too short ridge or an

asymmetric ridge. After that you will need skill, energy and luck to optimise the likelihood of your pup having dog show potential.

The assumption is that, primarily, you want the joy and pride of raising your dog or dogs. Therefore this chapter deliberately ignores the option of paying enough to buy you a proven adult show dog. If you do that you will either be buying a dog which, due to some tragedy, is for sale, or one which has been a kennel dog, and has not been closely loved and reared by its owner. I, personally, have little, if any, sympathy for the practice of raising and showing a dog in order to make it a Champion and then selling it for a great deal of money. Any Ridgeback that has been loyal enough to work with its master towards a Championship deserves a long after-show life with its closest companion and friend.

SHOW POTENTIAL
To be lucky means you need a combination of luck, energy and skills. Read all you can about the Ridgeback, so you can look for the right features in your potential puppies. Visit shows, learn to know which blood lines have produced higher-than-average show results. Some show stars might seem to fall almost from heaven, but there is a considerably larger chance that puppies from top-quality parents and grandparents will perform well. Show performance from parentage gives no guarantee, but it is a good start.

Some show stars win because they are exceptionally balanced. Some because they are extreme in some way, and compensating well for being, for example, just on the edge of being too tall, too small, too heavy or

Do not allow your heart to rule your head when assessing Ridgeback puppies.
Photo: Katja Volgelsinge, Austria.

too light. Sometimes the extreme quality is so positive that it overshadows a certain fault. In countries where written critiques of dogs shown in competition are made, your work is a lot easier. If there is a consistent fault mentioned in the critiques, then this is a warning signal. That unique "specialness" that has produced the show winner might not be inherited, but the slight fault might well be. Always look for the parents that show great balance and avoid extremes!

A few words about "types". If you are served tales such as "this is the African type", this is the "true old type", "this is the modern show type", the chances are that you are encountering a dog salesman you might not want to deal with. There are no "old" or "new" types of Ridgebacks – just individuals that conform to the Standards and individuals that do that to a lesser degree. The mere thought that we might accept deviations, or possibly even read the Standard with a bit more "fantasy" – not to mention the unmentionable, that the Standard may be changed to match traits that have occurred which are against the original Standard – is, and must remain, totally unacceptable.

CHOOSING YOUR PUPPY
You have learned about the breed, picked your breeder and your litter and now you look at the puppies.

48

Do not make a decision from your heart alone. There are many things you cannot see in a puppy. I assume that your arrangement is that you see the puppies from two to three weeks onwards, all the way to eight or ten weeks, and that you can still change your mind during the days before the delivery. There is a lot you can see and even feel in a young puppy.

Do not be taken in by the suggestion that a ridge that lacks two symmetric crowns, or one which is a lot narrower than those of its brothers or sisters, or which is too short in relation to the puppy's body length, will improve. It will never change for the better.

A marked lack of symmetry between skull and muzzle is a warning signal: so is a very broad skull at puppy age, especially in combination with a short muzzle. This could move towards becoming a coarse head.

Smallish paws and thin bone at the age of three to four weeks already signal the possibility that this will be a small, possibly even weak-boned individual. A puppy needs paws to grow into – or should I say paws to grow on to?

Feel with your fingers gently across the front of the puppy. If there is no little 'knob' at this age, there will not be a strong front. Do not believe the theory that 'the chest bone will develop'. You are more likely to be disappointed than not.

Colours are both easy and difficult. Too much white shows, and it will not disappear. Too much solid black outside the muzzle and ears should also be avoided; but this is a case where there could, sometimes, be changes. Black with silvery shades must be avoided, as they could turn into Weimaraner-coloured coats.

Dermoid sinus in the litter is controversial. As long as we do not know for sure that there are no hereditary elements, I would tend to warn against the choice of a dog from such a litter – especially as dogs with show potential are also, no doubt, potential breeding material.

5 CARING FOR YOUR RIDGEBACK

You have selected your puppy and have brought it home. Good contact and bad habits form dramatically during the first few days that a puppy spends in his new home. The advice to everyone who buys a dog for the first time is to be prepared both for long sleepless nights and to stand firm when your heart is breaking.

COMING HOME

The question of "no-go" territories in your homes has to be settled. Your bedroom or the computer room are good examples of such areas. Do not allow the puppy in, and, when he sneaks in anyway, use a simple command of your choice and move him out, gently and firmly. Ideally, find something else the puppy can be interested in. That is not difficult – everything in a new home is exciting.

There must be no punishments, because the puppy will have done nothing wrong. Wrong, in canine upbringing, only exists when your dog is breaking a rule you are sure the dog knows. At this stage, the new puppy will not know the rules.

Make sure your entire family speaks the same language, both in using a command, such as *not here*, with the same emphasis, and in body language and tone of voice. Mixed signals will confuse the puppy – and some months later the puppy will have learned to use those confusions skilfully to his own advantage.

The first nights might be short for you. The puppy has lost its mother, its litter mates and even the breeder's family. He or she will look for comfort and is likely to cry. This is the time when you need your determination, your steel will. The age-old trick for comforting a crying puppy is to place an old-fashioned alarm clock next to, or inside, a blanket within the puppy's bed. Another trick is to sacrifice some comfort during that first night and sleep on a mattress on the floor, next to the dog bed. I have heard stories about the master waking up on the floor in the morning with the puppy in the owner's bed. The will of steel is the best option! However, in addition to that unbendable firmness, it helps if you can buy the puppy's puppy-bed, the puppy's blanket and also some of the puppy's

Your puppy will probably feel lonely for the first few days.

particular pet toys from the breeder.

Make sure the puppy is given a guided tour around the home, to produce its own mental picture of this new, big world. The quicker the puppy dares to 'sniff around', the more open-minded it will be. It is also easier for it to learn the 'no-go' areas. For this purpose, make sure that a family member accompanies the puppy.

COMMUNICATION

Now the puppy knows its new home. Sooner that you would imagine, it has settled down, realising that this is all his or hers. This is the time to start communicating. This is, to use modern business terminology, total communication. Everything communicates: your voice, the way you say the commands, your body language, the slowness or swiftness of your movement. The thing that counts is – what

does the puppy experience in its own little mind?

You have chosen a Ridgeback and this means you have a dog which does not take easily to military-style commands. The dog will either begin to fear you, which is the worst of all starting points, or it will lose its respect for your leadership, which means it only follows your wishes when you are within touching distance, or it will, over time, become "deaf" to your commands. Your Ridgeback needs to know your rules and to respect you as a leader. For this you need to develop your own common language.

The first seven to twelve months are when you should learn to live with your companion and the dog should want to be part of your everyday life. This is not the time to start teaching more advanced canine activities.

It is your job to introduce your puppy to the outside world.
Photo: Liliane Volont, Belgium

The attention span of a Ridgeback is intense but short. When you train your dog, almost in play-form, remember that variation and repetition are equally important elements. Use short training periods, have fun, train for something else, have fun, train for a third issue, have even more fun – and then go back to the first training theme.

You should also do your best to learn how your individual dog reacts. Not only are breeds different from each other, individuals within the same breed can also vary tremendously.

LEADER NOT DICTATOR
A dog needs and deserves stability and this includes knowing whom to trust and whom to follow – the leader. It is to your and your family's benefit that the puppy accepts its position in the family early on. With very small children this needs, in certain cases,

some thinking out. Perhaps you should accept that the toddler and the Ridgeback puppy are more or less on the same level. Never, ever, lead a Ridgeback by force – and accept that you must teach the children in parallel with the dog. The dog has its basic rights, and there are more cases where children who have not been thoroughly guided have been a nuisance to a dog, than the other way round.

The best method of securing your role as the leader is to be the problem-solver, the nice guy without whom the puppy would find many things difficult, possibly even scary. In this way you will deserve the leadership, instead of trying to grab it by command. Later on, gradually move towards letting the puppy solve its own problems – even if it is trying to find the chewy bone from beneath the blanket, or straightening out the leash that is twisted around a lamp-post. Always, and that does mean always, give the puppy praise when it has solved a problem, and you will make sure that the puppy remembers it. Leadership means that the dog likes to obey and follow you, not that it has to follow you out of fear.

HOUSE TRAINING
A breeder who delivers puppies to their new homes after eight weeks cannot be expected to have got the puppies fully house trained. Eight or nine weeks is too early for this in the development of the puppies. However, the breeder can do a lot to help in this process.

Dogs are clean animals, but babies are babies and puppies are puppies and nature has decided that things have to take their own time. As soon as the puppies start moving around in the puppy box – with a certain degree of awareness about where they move – they should be offered a special corner for the calls of nature. The age-old, excellent solution is to save enough old newspapers for weeks ahead of the birth of the litter. These newspapers become the 'sand box' of the puppy area. They are easy to remove and replace and also to dispose of. The puppies will, amazingly quickly, start moving towards this special area. Naturally errors will occur. The rule is that the more frequently the puppy space is cleaned and the newspapers are exchanged for fresh ones, the faster the puppies will understand the meaning of cleanliness and the greater will be the urge to walk all the way from the warmth of the mother to the toilet area.

Once the puppies are big enough to be let out, you might use the trick of placing some newspapers just outside the house, or the kennels, on the sand or grass. In this way the puppies will associate going out with finding the toilet space. Otherwise they might run out in sheer joy, play and have fun, and suddenly run in again, like the obedient small dogs they are, to the paper in the puppy box!

In its new home, the now fast-growing puppy needs to be taken out frequently. For the sake of convenience, in the beginning, just let the puppy out as soon as it has been eating or drinking – or any time it shows restlessness. (This should stop by four to six months. See Nutrition). Speed is all-important and you want to offer as high a 'hit rate' for the puppy as possible.

A little later it is useful to start putting a leash on the puppy, in order to get it used to performing when being walked. Youngsters who have, all their lives, been used to running freely to the toilet will find it hard to do anything when walking on a leash. Soon this exercise should also be extended to grass (or sand) areas outside the home garden, so that the youngster gets used to being aired outside its own perimeters.

When the dog can be classified as a young adult, be aware that mistakes are still possible. Never think in the old-fashioned terms of penalising the dog when a mistake happens. Far too many times do we hear comments such as "you do that once more and I will put your nose into it". All you do is create an unpleasant situation for the dog, which cannot link it to the recent mistaken 'outing' indoors. The dog owner should never expose the dog to indignity.

On the other hand, if the young dog suddenly makes a habit of protesting against something by urinating indoors, then when, and only when, you can catch the dog in the act, you have to correct this behaviour gently but firmly. In addition, please try to understand what caused this behaviour. Lack of attention? Lack of contact and caring? If the cause might have been a scary noise or another unpleasant incident such as lightning, never punish the dog. Instead, if the source of the scare is within reach, take the dog on a leash, make sure you have optimal contact with it, and walk close to the source of the scare. Even in the case of lightning the dog normally feels OK if it can see the source or cause of its scare, by experiencing the lightning and thunder without the confinement of a house, but in the close vicinity of its master.

HOME ALONE

I take it for granted that you have never planned to leave the dog alone at home for entire days when you and your family are at work and school. To do that would be to fall well outside what can be considered good dog ownership. On the other hand, you must be confident that you can leave the dog alone for a little while, without worrying about either the dog's health or your own household. Start this training in the puppy's own environment. Let the dog stay alone for short periods, then return. Praise the dog when you return but avoid overdoing it. Do not teach the dog that when you come back you will always bring a goodie of some kind. This will make the dog's wait intolerably long and the dog will come up with the most creative ways to pass the time – the classic of chewing on shoes is just one in a million.

THE CAR AS A "SECOND HOME"

You should start training in your car very early on. It is a good thing to know that you can not only have your companion along with you on journeys, but that you do not need to worry about popping into the gas station or into the department store for some shopping.

There are two aspects to the puppy's "second home", the car. One is, simply, to make sure the puppy has no fears and feels at ease. The other is to train the pup to wait alone. Here exactly the same rules apply as for training your puppy at home.

In some countries it is almost a tradition to keep dogs in reasonably small cages which can fit into the back of a caravan or into a hotel room, for instance during dog show trips. Fortunately, in other countries excessive use of cages is considered to be mistreating the dog. It is a question of honour for any good dog owner that the relationship is such that the dog does not need to be locked into a small space such as a cage when the owner is away.

MENTAL STIMULATION

The Ridgeback, being a versatile breed, needs a lot of stimulation and a lot of variation. Invent your own games where the dog must solve small problems in a playful way. The varying training we discussed above is naturally part of the mental stimulation. But games such as hide-

The growing teenage Ridgeback needs short periods of training mixed with fun and play.

Photo courtesy: Susan Clayborough, Norway.

and-seek, scent discrimination, or playing with a ball are also important.

Meeting other dogs is essential training and is another way of stimulating your dog. The dog must learn early on to be in the company of other dogs. The young dog needs to learn 'doggie language' from older dogs. This is a fundamental essential for normal canine life. At the same time, the dog should also learn to know people. Not every human being is as enthusiastic about your new family member as you are, and the dog must understand this. Reading a 'normal' person is another must – especially as society seldom considers dog owners as being really normal! The dog must gradually learn how to cope with everyday life in the street. This is the bigger environment which the dog will, one day, have to master.

Make sure that you are nearby when your young puppy meets unfamiliar children for the first time. This is not the place for rough play from the children. You must never accept a child behaving badly with a dog, and especially with a puppy. At the same time, you are responsible for making sure that the playful puppy does not grasp a glove, or lick so that the child gets scared.

COLLAR AND LEASH
Lesson one is for your puppy to get used to a collar. Do not combine this with walking with a leash in the early stages; just teach the puppy to get accustomed to the collar.

Next, logically, you try the leash. Never force your puppy to walk nicely by your side during the first walks. The puppy needs to get used to the leash. If, or rather when, the puppy drags, give firm signals, like a clear but harmless pull. Do *not* drag

the puppy to your side, as it will not understand this behaviour.

I have an additional suggestion for the potential exhibitor. Teach the puppy to follow, wearing the leash, both running when you run and walking when you walk. Use a different command when you want it to run and another one when you want it to move back to a normal slow trot. When we say run, we mean fast trot: the idea of the entire exercise, which again must be seen as a game by your dog, is to prevent the dog from galloping when you run.

LEARNING TO SIT
When on the leash, train the puppy to sit. Push down gently with your left hand (you have, for this purpose only, moved the leash to your right hand, with the puppy still on your left side). Lift the puppy's head by the leash, gently, at the same time as you push the rump down and give the "sit" command. If you are a potential show enthusiast, you might choose, in your own language, another word than "sit", as it can happen that a competitor tries to disturb your dog in the ring through this common command. Never keep the puppy down by force. Also, when the dog is praised, be sure it stays sitting, or it will connect the praise with getting up rather than sitting down.

COMING ON COMMAND
The Ridgeback is a hunting dog. Even if it does not, as an adult, go to extremes in chasing animals in forests or the countryside, you must make sure it comes to you on command. This is, of all the commands, the real lifesaver. Teach the puppy to come to you from its own adventures in the 'wilderness' in your

Show training is best started outdoors. The main thing is to make sure the dog has fun – never mind the results at this stage.

Photo: T. Laurencikova, Slovakia.

garden or back yard, or some other fenced-in area. Use the same command time after time, frequently back off a bit when you give the command, and make sure the puppy is thoroughly praised when it comes to you. It is also essential that you do not accept the puppy just coming near you; the puppy must come close enough so that you are able to touch its collar.

EARLY SHOW TRAINING

When your puppy has been at home with you for some time the moment will come when your little Ridgeback can be taken out for short educational walks in the garden. Do not, at this stage, try to teach the puppy any serious show skills. The best qualities your puppy can learn at this age are to follow your gentle commands, to allow other people gradually to approach and to play with him and even to touch him lightly. You can start playing 'show the teeth' pretty early, as long as it only means fun and a play.

When the puppy is four to five months old you can start, through playing, to see if he or she will stand still for just a few seconds, upon a single command, on the leash. When I say a few seconds, I mean it

must not be more. The whole idea is to move towards a 'single command system' for future shows. Do not get used to the idea of manipulating legs and body position as this early age. Sure, your puppy would get used to it. And then he will still need it when he is, as a young adult, in his first shows.

Ideally, the dog stops and takes a pose from a special command given through the leash. Do not start serious show position training until the first shows are over. The most important point is never to have a showing machine, but a dog that loves going to shows. In between, as mentioned earlier, keep playing "run" (i.e. trotting) and "walk" games.

So, taking a puppy, for fun, to some puppy matches has the single objective of teaching it that this is a really enjoyable environment. The puppy learns that, when you do this together, you are in a good mood and the puppy gets extra attention and meets new friends. After that, and not before, you can start thinking in terms of adjusting small details, such as how the young dog positions its front or rear legs. But more of that later.

Never, ever, enter puppy shows to win. You will be tense, the puppy will not like it and you will have done the future show career of your Ridgeback a major disservice. Show training must be one of the really enjoyable plays in the puppy's early life.

THE YOUNG ADULT DOG

From the age of some thirteen months until at least two years old, the dog is gradually

Like all dogs, the Ridgeback needs a leader of his pack, and that is you, his owner. The Ridgeback must be trained by one single person, and the whole famiy must use the same terminology/commands.
Photo: M. Bernkopf, Austria.

changing towards adulthood. A Ridgeback bitch is likely to settle down after her second season, which is between about 17 and 20 months of age. The male looks very mature when approaching two years old, but mentally and even physically he is not fully developed until he is moving towards his third birthday. This does not mean that you could not meet Ridgebacks that look both reasonably-grown and mature at a year-and-a-half. Just do not expect them to behave in a fully mature way. The female normally reaches her pre-conditioned maximum height by nine to twelve months; the male can take a little more time. A dog of any breed will develop to its destined height without any nutritional "pushing". Nature does its job best when it is left alone to take care of the growth of a young animal of any species.

CONTROLLING BARKING

Young adult dogs sometimes like telling their neighbourhood about their existence. This is natural and part of the final maturing process. But barking dogs are a nuisance in modern society. Again, you need to be close to your dog, being able to control and, if need be, gently punish the dog, exactly when this unacceptable barking takes place. A water hose frequently comes in handy. A dog should be allowed to bark when it has a real reason – for instance, if it detects some unauthorised person moving in your garden. But 'joy barking' is what makes dogs less acceptable in society. Fortunately, Ridgebacks by nature are reasonably quiet and vocally controlled dogs.

PHYSICAL CARE

Your dog will need general hygienic care.

This is regularly done with puppies, but it is a rule that should last for all the life of the dog. A short-haired breed such as a Ridgeback does not need frequent showers unless the dog has run in dirty soil, been digging in smelly terrain, or rolled itself in such wonderful fragrances in the forest as elk or cow droppings. A thorough brushing with a not-too-hard brush is frequently enough. I assume, however, that your puppy was trained to like joining its master in the bathtub or under the shower. If this is not the case, then washing your Ridgeback is going to be a spectacular show!

Do not forget that the older the dog gets, the more tooth care it needs. Today you can buy special toothpaste for dogs. This might sound a bit overdone. It is not. Use a regular, or a special canine toothbrush, and make sure the dog's teeth stay white and free from stains. Giving the dog some big, hard bone to chew on is an additional help. Just check that the bone is not brittle – and that your dog's digestive system copes with it. You should remember that an adult Ridgeback does not only lick even the biggest bone, he or she is pretty effective in chewing it for food.

The nails need regular trimming. The dog suffers if it has to walk or run with long toenails. This is yet another habit that is best trained with a lot of patience and fun – and goodies, when the puppy is young.

The exercise bit is covered in other parts of this book. So are normal problems, such as ticks, or ensuring that the essential vaccinations are always in order.

NUTRITION

Now it is time to talk food, one of your Ridgeback's favourite topics! The decisive period for the Ridgeback in nutritional terms is in early youth. This is where the balanced diet is most crucial. It cannot be repeated frequently enough that the most common problem is over-feeding.

When we start to talk about adult Ridgebacks, we hope that your dog has avoided such unfortunate but rather common problems as Osteochondrosis. In clinical terms this means degen-eration in the deeper layers of the cartilage in the joints, leading to fissures, cracks and flaps of cartilage. This, in dogs, is most common in the elbows, shoulder, stifle and hock joints. It is hard to find high-class industrial foods on the market that are deficient in calcium. Problems tend to occur as the result of adding calcium and phosphorus-containing ingredients to already balanced food products).

For an adult dog, it does not matter if the owner chooses to produce homemade food or use industrial food. The international standards (NRC) give solid advice for any homemade food. A blend of three-quarters vegetable content, e.g. fibre-rich bread, corn and rice, with a quarter of animal products, i.e. quality meat, fish and eggs, will offer a diet with around 25 per cent proteins.

The minimum protein requirement, for an adult dog, per day, given in grams/day, is

Body weight	Grams/day
20 kgs	15.1
30 kgs	20.5
40 kgs	25.5
45 kgs	27.5

Body weight	Number of Eggs/day	20 per cent dry-matter cheese in grams/day	Beef in grams/day
20 kgs	2.25	170	90
30 kgs	3	230	125
40 kgs	3.70	285	155
45 kgs	3.50	310	170

Just to add to the 'security-check list' for those who prefer home-made food, this equals: (*See chart above*)

As far as industrial foods are concerned, there are two rules to remember.

All major brands produce goods based upon thorough research and the respective brands have decided on a given balance of ingredients. Do not rock this balance. Also, the dosages of the packs are there to be followed. It is not the fault of the produce if the dog owner underfeeds, or, which is much more common, overfeeds the dog.

Whether to choose industrial dry food based upon beef, lamb, chicken etc. is a question of personal choice – and testing with the individual dog or dogs. I have, for years, chosen to feed my show dogs with different dog foods, just because my experience is that dogs are pretty individual when it comes to finding the perfect nutrition.

A normal adult dry-food contains, on average:
Proteins 20-22 per cent; Fats 8-14 per cent, Calcium 1.1 per cent, Phosphorus 0.7-08- per cent and Sodium 0.25 per cent. These are indications in order to avoid pointing at a given brand.

With the above type of a complete dry-food in mind, daily rations should be around

A traditional question from new dog owners is "How many times a day should we feed the dog?" The most natural

Weight of dog	Dry-food in grams
20 kgs	320 grams
25 kgs	380
30 kgs	440
35 kgs	490
40 kgs	540
45 kgs	620

solution is to feed dogs twice a day, in the morning and in the evening. Contrary to the opinion of several experts, I recommend that dogs ought to have water available around the clock. A Ridgeback does not drink for fun but when it needs it.

When a Ridgeback is in heavy training, or just living a normal, active life in extreme conditions, e.g. severe cold, the daily need for nutrition is larger. During periods of heavy-duty exercise, for instance biking daily to get the dog into top show trim, you should consider the temporary use of a high-protein food.

ACUTE GASTRIC DILATION-TORSION
This is a life-threatening condition, also called Bloat. It is most frequent in the more mature dog and in large size, deep-chested dogs. It must be taken seriously by any Ridgeback owner. The most common cause is a large meal, followed shortly by exercise. Never let your dog roam freely until about one-and-a-half hours it has eaten!

The warning signals are clear. The dog

tries in vain to vomit, it becomes sad and restless at the same time because it is in serious pain and, if you tap the chest, you hear a drum-like echoing sound. The dog might also fall into shock after only a short time. This is when numerous changes in the body take place and the only solution is *immediate* veterinary help. We are talking about every single minute counting. The best chances offered to the dog are through surgery. The stomach must be decompressed and the stomach re-positioned.

If the dog owner wants to protect the dog, he keeps thorough control of the dog every day, after every meal. He can also take lessons in first aid. One helpful tool to have at home is a simple, steady plastic tube 1 metre in length, approximately one to one-and-a half centimetres in diameter. The bottom part should be closed (sealed by heat, for example) and next to the closed end a hole of about 1 centimetre in diameter should be cut. In a crisis situation this tube can be inserted through the dog's mouth all the way to its stomach, in order to buy the owner time to reach the vet, as this procedure will let out some of the gases from the stomach.

EXERCISE FOR BOTH
A Ridgeback which is not in good physical shape is not a true Ridgeback. If your dog is in bad condition it is not the dog's fault. On the other hand, do not, and I repeat not, start monotonous physical exercise such as biking before the Ridgeback is physically mature. Wait until the bitch has had her second season and, with the male, you should cool your eagerness at least until the dog is 18 months and, ideally, closer to two years of age.

Always keep in mind that moving freely puts a lot less strain on the dog than repetitive movements. Many Ridgebacks love running beside a horse. If you are a horseman, train your dog to be absolutely sure about obeying commands, and then enjoy nature. If you like jogging – and you are not training for a major competition – take your teenage Ridgeback along. The ideal is if you can let the dog run freely. Again, this is a question of the laws and regulations in the area where you live. Do not break the rules. Dogs are hunters, and Ridgebacks are fast hunters. We do not want to see newspaper articles about dogs "chasing" innocent joggers. For Ridgeback owners from more rugged climates, as some of the pictures in the book show, the good news is that the Ridgeback loves snow. Jumping around and playing in deep snow is not only fun, it is also great exercise.

When your Ridgeback is maturing, have a look at the possibilities of testing your dog in Lure Coursing. This, in short, is a lure (frequently a plastic bag type of thing) moving on a string just above the ground. In the US, the home country of this great sport, the long-track Lure Coursing imitates the full escape pattern of a running hare. In Australia you can test your dog with a shorter track. Some clubs, such as the Swiss club, also offer members a playful chance to test speed running on a greyhound track. More playful types of exercise include Flyball, which is especially charming done as a relay for teams and with young handlers. All these alternative sports offer the dog both mental and physical training.

Finally, back to basics. If you are just a normal dog owner, not an exercise freak, remember that walking – just normal, cosy strolls for three-quarters of an hour to an hour – is very sound training for both you and your dog.

WORKING WITH YOUR DOG

Working with your dog is one of the most rewarding aspects of dog ownership. Every dog owner is advised to take some classes, to read expert literature on, for instance, Obedience, and some slightly more advanced activities. Agility is one of my favourites, though the Ridgeback might be too enthusiastic to follow all the rules in detail. But it sure enjoys the action, which also helps develop balance and physical fitness.

There is no need to train your Ridgeback to carry out its guard duties on your property. The Ridgeback is a balanced, natural guard dog, which does not use more force than any situation would demand. Let your young Ridgeback live a normal life among people and among other dogs. Hopefully the moment will never come when you really need its guarding instincts and its ability to protect you or a family member. But, should that moment come, you can rest assured that you will be in good hands – or paws!

STOPPING BAD HABITS

Let us just return to a theme from the passage about the first hours and days the young puppy spends in its new home. It is not only puppies that learn bad habits. In the dog's eyes anything that is comfortable or tasty and not firmly and politely banned is smart. The adult dog will try new things. It could be sleeping in a sofa, sneaking up in the master's bed at night or stealing the cat food. It is your choice – either you are

firm, or the dog will move in the direction it has decided upon, not you. Watch out when you teach your young dog some tricks, such as 'swapping things'.

I once got home to a Ridgeback that was a master of swapping. That day, the chicken dinner was gone from the fridge, and instead I found one of my shoes. Fair deal, according to the young Ridgeback. The reason why this short story is not in the Anecdotes section (*Chapter Six*) is because it teaches a clear lesson here. Dogs are smart. They use what they learn – however the fact that the fridge door was closed tells still more about the strong tail of a Ridgeback than about its superb intelligence.

CANINE AGGRESSION

By the time your Ridgeback is a young teen we assume that the puppy training, teaching the dog to walk on a leash and to come to you on command are mastered. It is now the time to take some lessons with the firm objective of teaching your Ridgeback to walk by your side, without a leash. Just as when you started to train the puppy to come to you on voice command, you need to start this training in a safe place, free from nearby traffic. The best solution is to go to classes, as you then train your young dog in a proper environment with other dogs. The distraction that the other dogs provide is part of the final objective – to be able to control your dog in situations which you did not plan for. With dogs, just as with your own professional life, for example, planning and training is for the moments when the unexpected happens. Preparing for the expected is called common sense. In dog terms

Many clubs arrange Ridgeback walks. This is an excellent way of both exercising the dogs and teaching them to accept other dogs.

Photo: Di Jolly, Australia.

Biking is great training, not least for the show ring, as it teaches the dog to stretch out in long trot strides instead of galloping. Biking should never be started before the dog is fully grown.

Photo: Di Jolly, Australia.

Most Ridgebacks love following their owner when he or she is riding. The Ridgeback needs to be fully trained to obey commands before riding in or close to more densely populated areas.

Photo: Katja Vogelsinger, Austria.

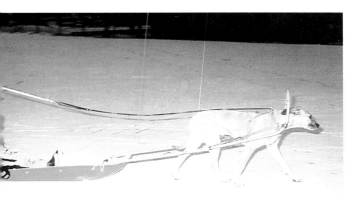

In the more Nordic countries, a midnight sledge-ride might seem far removed from Africa – the breed's native home – but in both Finland, Sweden and Norway Ridgebacks are often used for these outings.

Photo: Marianne Aaltonen, Finland.

Running free in the snow in between the sledge lessons is also fun.

Photo: Marianne Aaltonen, Finland.

Trekking the Norwegian way. Ridgebacks like carrying baggage when trained.

Photo: Susan Clayborough, Norway.

Agility is a sport tailormade for Ridgebacks who thrive on the speed and action.
Photo: Katja Vogelsinger, Austria.

Running the tunnel tests both speed and courage.
Photo: Mr Mosslar, Australia.

The Ridgeback excels at lure coursing.
Photo: Courtesy of Di Jolly, Australia.

Flyball is growing in popularity - another team game for Ridgback and owner.
Photo: Mr Mosslar, Australia.

There is no need to train your Ridgeback to carry out his guarding duties.

Photo: Katja Vogelsinger, Austria.

common sense is basic puppy training.

When with other dogs, do not tolerate your young dog answering the challenge for a little power game from other teenagers. Ridgebacks are not all that keen on starting trouble, but they are quick to react. Teenagers being teenagers, especially males, there is also a period when nature almost expects the young dogs to get their first experience of the battle for rank in the pack. The slightest sign of acceptance from the owner's side can be misread, and your dog will think you want it to show how strong it has grown.

Accepting any dog fight is wrong, because it will one day create trouble for the dog as well as for you. You can also be responsible for inflicting damage on other dogs. Remember that you own one of the most agile, fastest and smartest dogs, almost straight from nature. Furthermore, the Ridgeback's reputation in our society depends on how well its owners behave. No-one has the right to risk creating a bad reputation for a dog breed that does not deserve it. Should the worst happen and two dogs engage in a real fight – not a verbal contest – act swiftly in co-ordination with another dog owner or expert person. Both people must grab both the hind legs of each of the dogs simultaneously, lift up the hindquarters of the dogs, and drag them back just a little. No dog can bite you, or the other dog, when in this position.

MORE THAN ONE RIDGEBACK?
This is one of the big questions involved in owning dogs. Two dogs have much more fun together than one dog and its owner. Then, again, dogs defy mathematics insofar as owning two dogs is many, many times more complex than owning one dog. Having a pair gives the dogs mental stimulation even when the owners are not at home, or are busy. Dogs, not least Ridgebacks, are playful even when advanced in age, and can entertain and exercise themselves.

Remember, no matter how many Ridgebacks you own, they each require the same amount of love, care and exercise.   *Photo: Katja Vogelsinger, Austria.*

On the other hand, each dog in a couple needs as much exercise, love and devotion as a single dog. Assuming you want one dog of each sex, do remember that when your bitch is in heat, which is normally twice a year although Ridgebacks sometimes do have longer cycles, you will have to cope with separating the two dogs effectively for up to two weeks.

In the unlikely event that you end up with two dogs of the same sex, make sure they both respect you very strongly as the single leader. Then, make sure that they settle their internal ranking in a natural, non-violent way. Always remember that, if there is grumbling, your immediate duty is to calm it down by supporting the stronger dog, that is the pack leader among the dogs! Never feel so sorry for the "lower" individual that your behaviour is seen, by the dominant dog, as forming an alliance with the weaker one. Be equally loving with both, but show full respect for their internal balance of strength.

THE RESCUE RIDGEBACK
I hope that the vast majority of Ridgeback owners – indeed all dog owners – have had the privilege of seeing a puppy grow up in the family. But this is not always the case, and we should admire people who have chosen to select dogs from dog rescue shelters. A canine life saved is, in my view, a life saved – and life is not the only the most precious thing we have, it is the only thing.

In practical terms, if you take in a rescue dog it means that you bring a completely unknown factor into the home. It is sometimes almost impossible to know what horrible experiences the dog has suffered and what reaction these have left with the

dog. Special care must be taken when an adult dog is introduced to a family if there are children involved. If the dog buyer is not a person with significant canine knowledge and experience, then an experienced Ridgeback person should be asked to go along to the shelter to give advice.

The chances are that the new owner will be given some valuable indications about what to look out for. When taking in an adult dog, the first weeks must be entirely focused on socialising and getting to know the individual. Do not let the dog loose, unless you have an area with a high, secure fence. Never leave a child or children alone with this dog until you know that all parties understand each other.

Then, when your new dog has taken to you and your family as its wonderful new home, watch out for situations which the dog might read as threaten-ing, from someone or something from outside, to you or your family. It might want to protect you at all costs. Feel free to take your new, adult dog to dog clubs that offer dog walks in groups, and even basic obedience training. It is never too late to teach a dog new things! But, never, ever, give the dog away to a dog-training centre. You might not get a manageable dog back after that.

COMPANIONSHIP
When we were discussing the growing puppy we talked about how to train the dog to stay alone, both at home, for given periods of time, as well as in cars. It goes without saying that the old dog needs contact with his owners. Anyone who intends to buy a dog, which, as an adult, must spend over 4-6 hours per day alone,

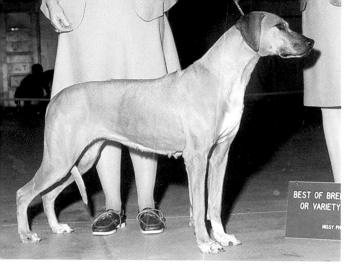

Well-cared-for Ridgebacks can live a long and healthy life. The US champion Rob Norm's Cee Gidget (Eilack's Tsumba of Kutari/Lionpride's Ruanda) won a major award at the age of 11 years and 6 months.

Photo courtesy: Joe Berger.

should quickly reconsider the decision. Cats are much easier to handle. What is essential, in addition, is not the 'home alone' or 'home with someone' question, but the sheer ownership attitude. A dog can be very alone in a family which works from its home and seldom leaves the place. It is a nice habit to talk to your companion, pat him now and then and remember that he is really part of your family.

When you take your Ridgeback out for its daily walks and its physical exercise, remember that, again, it is not exercise alone your dog needs, but exercise, friendship and fun. In countries with a civilised attitude to dogs in public places, it is always a joy to see how dogs learn to accompany the families for a Sunday lunch or dinner in the village restaurant. This assumes that the dog is under full control and trained to behave among other people and, frequently, a number of other dogs.

Companionship also means fairness. Even if you have had a bad day, do not take it out on your dog. He is innocent. In fact, he is sometimes the best friend you have, because he will never question your wisdom, just always offer you his unquestioned loyalty.

THE VETERAN RIDGEBACK

Even if a Ridgeback is a sizeable dog, it is also a natural, sound animal. A dog which has had its fair share of physical exercise, plus sound owner and companion contact, will stay active until well advanced in years.

I believe the biggest disservice you can do to a dog that is approaching veteran age – for the sake of picking a time-line, let us say between six or seven – is to pay less attention to the dog, give it less mental stimulation and take it out less.

As a veteran, the Ridgeback no longer plays so long with younger dogs and there is a need for the owner to take his or her share of the responsibility. The mentality of a Ridgeback remains playful and sound. There is little risk that an ageing dog would be more easily irritated and short-tempered, for instance with foreigners or children. This is, naturally, assuming that the dog is healthy and does not suffer from pain.

The privilege of owning a Ridgeback makes it a matter of honour for any friend and owner of the breed to be close to his companion exactly as long as the dog's life lasts. A true Ridgeback will be remembered long after that.

6 THE RIDGEBACK IN SOCIETY

Ridgeback behaviour has, in expert texts, been described in many ways, such as alert, aloof, arrogant, avoiding danger, conflict-shy, devoted, independent, and self-sustained.

All of these words contain a large grain of truth. The challenge is to describe the complexity of Ridgeback behaviour and also to anticipate the Ridgeback reactions. In the early chapters we have seen examples of behaviour in situations which are likely to occur in one form or another and in which the Ridgeback is pretty likely to follow the prescribed pattern.

Below, the reader will find an attempt by a professional behaviour expert to assess the Ridgeback's reactions to various stimuli, in comparison with other dog breeds.

This is a mapping exercise, not an attempt to describe 'good' or 'bad' qualities in relation to the average. In order to offer a "soft values" description of Ridgebacks, this scientifically serious chapter is followed by true stories, in the shape of anecdotes. No picture of a typical Rigeback is complete without a combination of research and real life.

ANTI-DOG SENTIMENTS

Today's society is not developing in positive directions when judged from a canine viewpoint. Ironically, the role of dogs in human society is now more varied than ever before in the history of the human and canine bond. Dogs serve us as guard dogs, as narcotics dogs, as landmine searching dogs, as avalanche dogs, as military dogs, as rescue dogs, as mould-searching dogs, as mushroom-searching dogs, as mine dogs, as guide dogs, as service dogs for the handicapped, and in many other fields.

Yet, with the urban expansion in the industrialised countries, with new virtual realities and play-worlds, with new hobbies and sports, with the human mind distancing itself from its own roots as a healthy, natural being, not only have dog registration figures taken a dip but sensational journalism has blown up 'dog scares' to abnormal proportions. Cynical politics in countries with real problems, such as unemployment or social violence, sometimes tend to introduce easy, symbolic legislative action. Canine rights have been seriously threatened by these developments.

To give just a few concrete examples: even in Australia there are mathematical formulae for having dogs in city environments; in Southern France – the dog-loving country in Europe par excellence – there are bans on dogs in city centres; and dogs have been banned from ships and ferries, trains, underground trains and buses. Germany has introduced penal taxation for some breeds; and many countries e.g. Belgium include Ridgebacks on lists of "dangerous dog breeds". It is increasingly hard, when travelling with dogs, to be accepted in hotels and restaurants; dog shows have been cancelled because of the threat of 'allergy problems'. In one country there is a proposal to force dogs to be walked on a leash even in the owners' own fenced-in back yards.

MISUNDERSTANDING RIDGEBACKS
Our own breed is listed among 'fighting dogs' that must wear a muzzle in some German states, as well as in Ireland.

The German situation is particularly tragic, as there are official statistics analysing police reports of alleged dog problems over a five-year period. The total number of Ridgebacks involved during this five-year period in any sort of problem is *eight* – a very low figure, in a total of 8,000, particularly when compared with the behaviour of many other breeds. And this has to be judged against the fact that Germany is a major Ridgeback country in Europe.

The problem is the misunderstanding created by the old name 'Lion Dog', and the false idea that Ridgebacks would have hunted and, by themselves, attacked and killed lions.

The proud guardsman. The guarding qualities were the other early feature that made the ridged dogs, and later the Ridgebacks so popular on the farms in South Africa. In this respect, nothing has changed. The Ridgeback is a natural, reliable guard dog, which does not go to excesses when action is needed.   Photo: Georg Marek, Germany.

It goes without saying that all Ridgeback owners, as well as clubs, have a major communication challenge ahead of them. It is equally clear that we must expect Ridgeback owners to take basic training seriously, and we must expect anyone who breeds even a single Ridgeback litter to exercise absolute care when selecting their puppy buyers. The Ridgeback lovers alone cannot tackle the overall canine problem. Some countries, notably Sweden, have taken action at Kennel Club level, starting ambitious and far-reaching communication campaigns. These include advertising and

Cars and property are safe with a Ridgeback in the neighbourhood. He is a controlled, non-aggressive, yet firm guardsman.

political briefings, as well as educational programmes in schools, to rectify the misconceptions about dogs in general.

TRUE RIDGEBACK BEHAVIOUR

In the introductory remarks to the temperament section at the World Congress in 1996, I made two strong points: that we have to see the difference between "temperament" and "behaviour", and that we should chart more scientifically Ridgeback breed-specific behaviour.

A number of countries have introduced obligatory mental tests, under various names, to test dogs, for instance for breeding suitability. In some cases, for example in France, the test is even linked to the French Championship. I wonder why the very able French show judges have not objected. This rule can easily be seen as a criticism of their ability to assess social behaviour in the show ring.

All testing of dogs started from an ambition to select individuals for very specific purposes, such as military, or guard dog use. The early dog tests took a strictly functional approach, assessing

competencies, which could have been either inherited or learnt. The environments were in most cases reasonably identical, for instance in military dog schools, and results show that the trainers/breeders over time managed to predict, for instance, 'courage' and 'trainability' (fast learning of clear commands) successfully.

This book does not attempt to go into dog psychology, which normally means therapeutic analysis. However, I do give one single piece of very serious advice: if a dog has mental imbalances, for instance because of abuse, the last thing to do is to take this individual through the traditional 'temperament test'. It will, in all probability, destroy the poor dog. Use a skilled behaviour expert who can make judgements about the environmental causes of the trouble.

BEHAVIOURAL DESCRIPTIONS

The Swedish Kennel Club experimented for a number of years with a mandatory, simple 'mental check' (Mentalprov) as a pre-condition for Championships. After some years, realising that little benefit came out

In order to understand how the Ridgeback works in nature you need to work with your dog in free terrain, ensuring that it is under your control and supervision. A Ridgeback has, as the Swedish expert Eva Bryntse has noted, a remarkable skill of registering and following multiple happenings simultaneously. Photo courtesy: H. Tandefelt.

of the tests, with the exception of some income for the arranging clubs, the tests were abandoned, and wisely so. On the other hand, in retrospect, the advantage was that the test staff had acquired significant knowledge of many different breeds. With much more advanced testing continuing on a voluntary basis in Sweden, we can today fall back upon lessons learnt both through these mass checks and more serious testing programmes.

The test judge Barbro Börjesson, from the internationally renowned Sollefteå Dog School (a former military establishment), has for years co-operated with the Swedish Ridgeback Club, which has actively promoted testing, again on a voluntary basis. She has helped put together a grid, analysing similarities and differences in average Ridgeback behaviour, in relation to the overall averages.

Her background comments include some noteworthy remarks, such as the idea that Ridgeback owners have excelled in interest in temperament-related issues. (Ms Börjesson has now tested 58 Ridgebacks,

which is a solid start for comparisons with other breeds.) She feels that the Ridgeback is an "easy and stable breed, showing interest in hunting without excesses". The Ridgebacks have not been over-keen on grabbing prey with the mouth. She says that the "Ridgebacks show a light, threatening behaviour when challenged, with well-balanced aggression." She feels that "Ridgebacks are relatively weak and the courage gives in rather easily." She has also wondered if the breed has "a hereditary disposition for disliking gun shots".

"Ridgebacks are not easily impressed by strangers," she also notices as a plus point. She feels that, taking the average of a variety of dogs, there are fewer easily stressed, "locked-up" Ridgebacks. Her closing recommendation, because so many Ridgeback owners had understood the intentions of the tests, was that Ridgeback clubs should formally train test judges.

In attempting to translate the result grid, it seems that most of the judges' views appear to be accurate, in relation to what we want. However, the Ridgeback's inherited avoidance of risks is incorrectly seen as a lack of courage. This confusion is understandable, as head-on responses are required among, for instance, military and police dogs. The gunshot reactions are presumably the result of few owners training their dogs to the gun today, especially those living close to city centres. Gunshot steadiness can have hereditary elements, but just like ninety-nine per cent of the so-called Ridgeback 'temperament tests' which some clubs have invented, these test elements are a case for training.

This comparison uses the 29 Ridgebacks tested in the year 1996. The main number shows 1996 cases; the parenthesis shows the previous number of detected cases of each behaviour.

APPROACHABILITY ELEMENTS (INTEREST IN UNKNOWN PEOPLE)
Unreliability – shows social signals but is aggressive. NO.
Aggression – rejects contacts by aggressive behaviour. NO.
Reserved – retreats, shows insecurity. (1) 0
Less approachable – does not answer contact attempts. (7) 10
Open and approachable – balanced, easy to get in contact with. (19) 19
Overly open – Intense search for contact. NO.

HUNTING-RELATED FIGHTING INSTINCTS (INTEREST IN PURSUIT, INTEREST IN PREY)
Lack of interest. 1
Low interest. 8
Small interest. (6) 7
Medium – quick to follow, low interest in prey. (17) 8
High intensity, interested in prey. (3) 5
Very high – much intensity, no interest in prey. NO.

SOCIAL FIGHTING INSTINCTS (TENDENCY TO FIGHT WITH OR AGAINST SOMEONE)
Lack of interest. 2
Low interest – hard to involve in fighting situations. (4) 4
Small interest – responds late to fighting invitations. (15) 17
Medium – answers distinctly to invitations to fight. (8) 16
High – invites to fights without reason. NO.
Very high – intense in fighting, hard to call off. NO.

TEMPERAMENT (ADAPTABILITY AND CURIOSITY)
Lazy and unexcited – not interested in test situation. NO.
Somewhat lazy – hard to get started, slow. (1) 3
Less excited – slow to get started, then often lively. (12) 8
Lively – curious and adaptable. (13) 17
Very lively – frequently disturbed by environment. (1) 1
Impulsive – changes activities constantly. NO.

SHARPNESS (TENDENCY TO GET ANGRY WHEN THREATENED)
Shows none. (1) 0
Low tendency – few aggressive signals, only in some situations. (5) 1
Small tendency – aggressive signs without weight. (7) 6
Medium – balance and emphasis in reaction. (13) 13
Significant – in general, excessive aggression. 5
Unrelenting aggression – aggressive after threat disappeared. NO.
Note: 4 hard to judge (2)

DEFENCE INTENSITY (WILLINGNESS TO DEFEND ITSELF)

Shows none. (3) <u>0</u>

Low willingness – tries to scare off, backs away, gives up. (4) <u>5</u>

Small willingness – replies with hesitation or awaits next steps. (9) <u>12</u>

Medium – answers with firmness, does not back off. (11) <u>7</u>

Significant – rejects attacks with power, attacks itself. <u>1</u>

Exceptional – rejects without reason, uncontrolled. <u>NO.</u>

NERVOUS CONSTITUTION (BASIC STRESS LEVEL, CONCENTRATION AND RELAXATION ABILITIES)

Stable – can get involved, fully unconcerned, no stress signals. <u>1</u>

Relatively stable – reliable and balanced, could show a few wrong signs. (10) <u>11</u>

Some tendencies of nervousness – some problems in concentration, problems in relaxing or few wrong reactions. (9) <u>11</u>

Somewhat nervous – several wrong reactions, stress level can increase cumulatively. (6) <u>2</u>

Nervous – in general too high stress level, difficulty in relaxing. (2) <u>1</u>

Significantly nervous – problems with concentration, abandons test. <u>3</u>

HARDNESS (ABILITY TO FORM MEMORY PICTURES)

Very hard – totally untouched and independent. <u>NO.</u>

Hard – usually untouched, independent. <u>NO.</u>

Medium hard – forgets fast, no disturbing independence. (2) <u>2</u>

Somewhat weak – shows memories but is not disturbed by these. (9) <u>9</u>

Weak – remembers well, can be subservient. (13) <u>16</u>

Very weak – disturbed by memories, subservient. (4) <u>2</u>

ABILITY TO ACT (CAN OVERCOME FEAR)

Non-existent – cannot overcome even with assistance. (1) <u>3</u>

Weak – reluctant to overcome despite assistance. (12) <u>9</u>

Limited – can overcome some situations by itself. (11) <u>12</u>

Medium – overcomes, sometimes with assistance. (3) <u>4</u>

Significant – overcomes with rare extra time needed. <u>NO.</u>

Very significant – overcomes fast and independently. <u>NO.</u>

Note: 1 hard to judge.

GUN SHOT STEADINESS (REACTIONS TO GUN SHOTS)

No reaction. <u>NO.</u>

Reaction that vanishes. (18) <u>16</u>

Small reaction each time. (3) <u>7</u>

Lowered activity level. <u>NO.</u>

Increased activity level. <u>NO.</u>

Scared, wants to avoid. <u>1</u>

Note: 5 did not participate (6) <u>0</u>

I suggest that it would be essential to find a uniform format for comparing Ridgeback behaviour with other breeds. This format ought to take into account the historical descriptions of the functions performed by the early Ridged dogs and it should be easy and clear, in order to avoid the eternal problem of translating test forms into different languages and cultures.

RIDGEBACK MEMORIES

Writing about dogs, covering Breed Standards, giving advice on health and training matters, discussing how to achieve sound dog nutrition or assessing mentality testing tends to end up, sooner or later, in too many facts and figures. It must be remembered that ultimately the relationship between a human being and a dog is a very emotional one. The intention of this section is to give the soft side of dog ownership a chance. It is said that the role of journalism is to make the important interesting. The ambition here is to make the intangible memorable.

I once wrote that "I have never accepted memories as substitutes for optimism and ambition." On the other hand, and with 15 more years of hindsight (or is it sheer age?) I want to add that memories can be the best source of inspiration to get the energy to stay optimistic and forward-looking. Hence these anecdotes.

NO SMILES
Does a dog have a sense of humour? Well, it is questionable. However, it can definitely show clear disapproval of what human beings think is funny. Years back my wife and I took our then 'superstar', Loustigens Douglas, to a show in Finland. Together with some colleagues and competitors, and also with a number of Ridgeback males playing correctly together, we walked in the young, green, spring countryside. Then we found something that everyone thought was great fun, letting the dogs jump back and forth across a small river. Few things are so elegant as Ridgebacks running and jumping. Someone said they can almost "fall effortlessly upwards." Everything went well, until Douglas slipped in the now muddy grass and fell into the river. Everyone cheered – and we laughed. It was a wet and sour dog that walked back to the motel, with an almost visible grey cloud over his head. The real lesson came the next day at the show – this legendary show winner refused to show at all. No aggression, just no humour, either. So much for laughing at your dog when he needs sympathy!

THE IMPROMPTU HERDSMAN
The following story was told to me by Lobo's owners, Mr and Mrs Fitzboegel. Apparently they were taking Lobo to a German club show, and during the trip they stopped to let the dogs out. They found a

The Ridged guard: Trespassing no doubt impossible.

Photo: Rens Trappel, Netherlands.

large grass area, and though they normally always kept their dogs on the leash, knowing that they always obey a command, they felt they could let Lobo run free for a few minutes. This proved to be a wrong decision. Some hundred metres away was a fenced-in area with 11 calves in it. The next five minutes were the longest in the Fitzboegel's lives. Lobo had decided to go deaf and run into the fenced area, through dense barbed wire. He then started to run around the calves, skilfully avoiding all attempts by the disturbed animals to kick him. When the Fitzboegels reached the fence, the 11 calves had been elegantly herded into one single, tight unit. None of the calves was hurt, not even touched.

Once they had solved the problem of getting Lobo out again unharmed through the barbed wire, the Fitzboegel's reflected on the fact that a Ridgeback which had never seen a cow in his life still had the old instincts intact – including those of an extremely competent herding dog.

INDEPENDENT VUMBA
Mariette van der Veer and Rens Trappel, owners of the great Champion Vumba and of Jessie, have travelled the world extensively through their love of Ridgebacks and have some charming anecdotes.

When Vumba and Jessie were still quite young, two and one years old respectively, Mariette took them with her to the hospital where she works because her colleagues wanted to see them. She let them out of the car at a side entrance to the hospital. While people were petting Jessie, Vumba went to the entrance, the automatic glass doors opened at his approach and into the hospital went Vumba. Mariette hurried to put Jessie back into the car and ran after Vumba. In the meantime he had entered the ward of Internal Medicine, had jumped onto the bed of one of the patients and was settling down. The patients were all amazed, and Mariette took Vumba off the bed and apologised. This was Vumba's short career as Doctor Vumba, as he was known ever afterwards in the hospital."

In 1993 Mariette and Rens took Vumba and Jessie with them on holiday to Israel. They were staying at the Sea of Galilee and went out to dinner one evening with Israeli friends. The dogs were not admitted to the restaurant because they were too big, so they were put in the 4x4 car with the windows open. As the party were starting their dinner they heard people around them talking about two dangerous dogs who were walking in the streets – in fact emptying the streets. They went outside and then saw Vumba and Jessie having great fun, with all the people running way. They put them into the car once again, put them on their leads and tied them up securely. Then minutes later, as they were continuing dinner, complete silence fell in the restaurant. Vumba had opened the door and entered the restaurant. He stood there, looked all around, and then saw them. He made a run for Mariette and Rens, dropped down under Mariette's seat, and remained there for the rest of the evening. Nobody dared to remove him after this incident. He had a very happy time – having bitten through his leash in the car.

DOG OF THE DAY
Jessie was the star of the next story, which happened when Rens and Mariette took four Ridgebacks with them on holiday to France. On the way there they went to a show. After the judging they were told to be in the Main Ring at 4:00pm with Vumba and Chirembo. So they put the other two dogs, Vizara and Jessie, into the kennel together with their bags containing their camera, video, wallets, credit cards and all their money. They did that because Jessie did not like people she did not know.

While they were walking around the grounds they heard a message on the paging system that there was a Rhodesian Ridgeback in the Main Ring. They wondered who would let their dog loose like that but, because it was not yet time for them to go to the Main Ring, and they knew they had secured their dogs properly, they stopped for a glass of champagne. An hour later another message came through the paging system saying that the Ridgeback was still in the Main Ring and would the owners please collect it. Rens gave Chirembo and Vumba to Mariette and went back, just to check, to where they had left Jessie and Vizara in the kennels.

To Rens's great surprise Vizara had managed to open the kennel from the inside and had escaped – to go into the Main Ring. In the meantime Jessie had remained in the kennel and was guarding their property. People had tried to close the kennel door, but Jessie had not permitted even that. She was truly dog of the day, even though the two others managed to get a CC. Sometimes, Mariette and Rens felt, being a dependable Rhodesian Ridgeback (with only one crown) meant more than being just a show dog.

VIZARA THE LION DOG
One day Mariette was taking Vizara for a walk by herself because she was in season. As Mariette was driving to the Nature

True canine partnership.

Photo: Katja Vogelsinger, Austria.

Photo: Katja Vogelsinger, Austria.

Reserve where she was accustomed to walking the dogs she saw an odd-looking man. When she was walking with Vizara she noticed that he was following her, and there were canals on either side of her, trapping her on her path. She grew pretty scared, as Vizara is the smallest of their Ridgebacks and she did not have a mobile with her. Her adrenaline level rose steadily, but when the man started to attack her, Vizara was there, all of a sudden, with bared teeth. She nibbled the attacker, who ran off. Mariette says she has never been so grateful to Vizara and has no doubts whatsoever concerning the matter of height. Its the spirit that counts!

THE MOST WANTED AMERICAN

Dr Pamela Rosman founded the Samara kennel in the USA. One day the Ridgeback she had bred called Samara Kwamira, who was four years old, tall and around a solid 90 pounds, had gone missing. Samara Kwamira was known as Madison and his owner, Julie Sutherland, was so devoted to him that he accompanied her down the aisle at her wedding.

Dr Rosman distributed some 1000 flyers, describing Madison. She called in two pet psychics. The Nassau district police were asked to bring in helicopter support. People who made home deliveries, such as Federal Express, UPS and all regional post offices were briefed. Finally she called upon all churches on North Shore, asking them to mention Madison in their Sunday services.

Six days after the search had begun, a post-carrier saw a dog behind a house and called Mrs Sutherland. Having raced to the area, she started calling for the dog from the highest position she could find. It still took a while, but eventually Madison appeared – having convinced himself by that time that there were no lions in the area!

As Dr Rosman said afterwards: "If you lose your dog, you do not just sit down and worry. You work until you find him!"

THE FLYING RIDGEBACK

According to Randi Jo Turken, "You can always tell a Ridgeback from a mile away. If it is male, the dog looks like a regal lion. Pure muscle as well as elegance. If it is female, the dog is sleek and muscular with an equestrian gait." One of the reasons why Randi, of New York's Upper West Side, decided to get a Ridgeback was because of their ability to go long, long distances. She jogged six miles every morning and how Charlie loved that run! "She was such fun to watch," said Randi, "there was sheer joy on her face when her long, lean, muscular legs flew through the air. And to all the squirrels in her path – beware. She raced towards them at full speed and then leapt five feet in the air to try to head off the squirrel as it scurried up a tree." Charlie died in the fullness of time, but when Randi got married, Whitney Houston's song "I will always love you" was played at the wedding, dedicated to the memory of Charlie.

7 SHOWING RHODESIAN RIDGEBACKS

Dog shows fulfil at least three different functions. The judging is, or at least should always be, based upon the individual qualities of each dog, ahead of any competitive judging. Different countries offer different formats. From a cynological standpoint the show formats which offer quality assessment, with a written critique of each individual dog, are no doubt the most constructive.

Second, shows have a combined educational and social function. They should bring people together – some of them expert breeders, some hobby exhibitors, some new enthusiasts and those interested in studying a breed. What is happening in the ring is essential to those outside the ring. At the same time, the atmosphere both inside and outside the ring must be positive, in order to facilitate an exchange of ideas and views. 'High elbowing', either symbolically or, heaven forbid, literally, is always detrimental to the breed in question. In countries where judges are encouraged to give an open critique the educational aspect functions at its best. Personally, I believe that judges

who cannot publicly handle the assessment and subsequent placing in a show ring should not judge. Equally, show systems where open critique is not allowed should be critically scrutinised. Is there a single real reason for not promoting open critiques (except for possibly disliking truth in public)?

Finally, there is the sporting, or call it competitive element to a dog show. This also fulfils a function, though competitiveness regularly is questioned. Competitions stimulate effort, and effort in turn motivates people to try harder. In a correct dog show environment, the atmosphere, the very air in the ring and the ethical rules of the game are also an education. We cannot function in any society unless we know how to improve, and equally, how to accept defeat and how to learn from the harder lessons.

UNDERSTANDING SHOW DOGS
The best education for anyone keen on starting a show career is to study winning dogs. When discussing buying a "show puppy" we noted there are no such

animals. There are dogs with "show potential".

Then, again, when looking at winning adult Ridgebacks there are lessons to be learnt, but in the end, the only person who can teach you enough is you yourself. Watch dogs, compare them, and assess why you think you prefer one top dog to another. The word I use is *why*. There is no such thing – and especially not for a show judge – as "I like". There has to be a reason behind a decision. The reason has to be linked to functionality. Though the saying is a bit harsh, I always remember a person who said to a younger colleague "I am not interested in what you think or feel, I just want to hear what you know." Knowing, in canine terms, means

UNDERSTANDING DOG SHOWS
Results and, consequently, levels of excellence, are measured in centimetres, metres, seconds or even hundredths of seconds in many sports. There is also a sports aspect to dogs. In some modern sports, for instance Lure Coursing or Agility, if the tracks were fully standardised we would, presumably, one day make comparisons. It is already interesting to compare the performances of different breeds in Track Racing and Lure Coursing, not so much to establish an order of supremacy between the breeds, but to add to the understanding of the breed-specific qualities.

In contrast, classic dog shows produce heroes and heroines which can never be fully compared from one continent to another, as we cannot easily – if at all – show our dogs globally. Even less so should we imagine that we could compare great show dogs from different periods. Dog shows themselves have changed, for the benefit, and in some cases the detriment, of canine development. Showmanship and handling play a bigger role today than even ten years ago. In some countries this has led to the extreme that a dog is, virtually speaking, doomed unless it is shown by a professional handler. In addition, the show grounds have changed dramatically, mostly for the better.

New ultra-elitist competitions, the various Champion of Champions and Supreme Champion extravaganzas, have given rise to a new breed of handlers, who train their dogs until the pair work as one inseparable entity. Remembering that the ultimate criterion for judging Ridgebacks is that they are as natural and as close to Nature and their African heritage as possible, we should still not even pretend to be able to compare qualities between different ages and generations. Knowing, in canine terms, means understanding how a dog functions, understanding the specific behind a special breed, being able to read the Breed Standard, and then having the skill to link what you see (or feel with your hands) to the functional background. Consequently, a dog show is not a beauty contest but a competition based upon evaluation of soundness in relation to the Breed Standard of a dog breed, plus general physiological canine knowledge.

LEARNING HOW TO SHOW
We assume that your Ridgeback was taken to some shows as a puppy, and that the dog really had fun at these events. You

When your Ridgeback is about 4-5 months old, you will already be able to assess show potential. This youngster indicates it will have a wonderful body length, and probably good angulation. The front is sound; the hindquarters have still to develop. The head is narrow when viewed from the front, but this is a good sign as it is unlikely to become too broad. Importantly, the alert expresssion is clearly eviden. Photos: U-B. Persson.

might already have started with the technique of always changing to a special show collar when the ring steward asks the dog to come to meet the judge. This will teach the dog that there is something special about a show.

More serious showing starts and ends with your ability to understand the quality of your own dog. The idea of competitive dog shows is to show honestly, but expertly, the strong sides of your dog in the best way you can. This means that a dog owner who refuses to see the weaker sides in his or her dog is less likely to be able to accentuate the strong sides.

LEARNING TO LOSE

Remember that you will never win all your shows, even if you are fortunate to have a star Ridgeback. Winning does not make the losers lesser Ridgebacks, and losing does not take anything away from your wonderful companion. As in all sports, the basic requirement is sportsmanship. Congratulate the winners. Accept congratulations when you win. But do not lose your perspective. Being a good sportsman does not mean neglecting the reasons for losing. The other dog was better. Fine. You were equal, but the other handler was better. Take this as a challenge, learn and train.

Judging the ridge quality is possible a few minutes after a puppy is born. The proportion of the length to the body, as well as the symmetry will never change. When evaluating a ridge it is imperative that there are two – and only two – crowns symmetrically opposite each other. Even experienced judges sometimes fail to judge another criterion, i.e. the length of the ridge. This is an example of a sound ridge expected from a Champion.

TEAMWORK

Be a team with your dog. The most sensitive moment is not when you need to show your dog standing still, it is when you show the dog in motion. A Ridgeback at its best is a glorious mover, one of the most beautiful among all dog breeds. Make sure you can move at all speeds without the dog losing the trot. This, again, can and should be trained. If you have a good-moving dog, make sure you wait with your run until you have enough space in the show ring. If the judge runs the entire class, you need to have a dog that concentrates on you, not on chasing the dog ahead of it, otherwise this eventually ends up in a gallop and a loss of rhythm and presentation.

When showing your Ridgeback standing up, do not let your hand movements show your possible worry. Never correct a weak part of your dog when the judge is watching. If you run into a crisis, with your dog standing in an unfortunate posture, take the dog around you and re-position it. Remember that standing up well always starts from the front legs being at an absolute 90-degree angle to the ground. Talk to your dog. If the dog has a great expression, try to get the dog to watch the judge with alert curiosity in its eyes when the judge passes by the line-up of dogs.

Finally, if you are meeting some unfairness in the show ring – and it can happen, even if the Ridgeback rings generally have been less exposed than some really competitive breeds – keep your cool. If you get upset or nervous your dog notices it before you do yourself. The ring stewards are there to make sure each dog is shown under equal and fair conditions. Do

Assessing the general composition of a Ridgeback is best done in medium-fast gait. The head is still carried over the topline (this will change in fast trotting, when the neckline is lowered to the level of the topline). The tail-root is parallel with the ground (anything else signals a less-than-perfect croup), and the tail is set slightly lower than the topline (which would be a fault). The strides are long and effortless, with the paws almost caressing the ground (high, front paws, as an example, indicates an incorrect front, presumably due to a straight shoulder). Also pay attention to the long, lean muscles of the hind legs. Short, round muscles give explosive speed over short distances – but a Ridgeback is a long-distance runner.

not be too shy to ask for assistance, for instance in removing dogs that are hanging around in, or too close to, the ring. And remember to hug and praise your Ridgeback, whatever happened on a certain day in the ring.

SHOW EQUIPMENT
All the above is about the showing in the ring. Your show dog also deserves to get the best conditions possible outside the ring. Do not forget a soft, warm blanket to put under the dog. If the show is held outdoors and you are not yet at the stage when you have purchased a show tent, at

least bring a big sunshade. Water is an absolute must – my dogs all drink one particular brand of bottled water! If the show rules demand that the dog is kept in a show cage, bring along a lock for the box, so that you can be sure the dog as well as your valuables stay in the box if you need to move around a bit. Remember that the show is supposed to be fun for the dog. Do your best to avoid leaving the dog alone for long periods. And do keep up a warm dialogue with your dog during the entire show. Finally, you did check and pack the entry ticket and the catalogue number of your dog, didn't you?

8 *WHAT MADE THEM GREAT?*

Just as we have sports heroes, there are famous as well as less well-known individuals in the canine world. The Ridgeback annals have their own heroes. This chapter presents a few of them, for the single purpose of honouring those individuals which have done great things in the show ring.

MAKING THE CHOICE

I have attempted, with this 'gallery' of great Ridgebacks, to base my comments on first-hand experience and information. Numerous individuals, which presumably are equally qualified, possibly even more qualified, have not been included. In most cases, their merit lists tell the full story of their show careers, and victories won are merits forever. While I have no conscience, as an author, about making decisions or statements some people might not like (that is also part of life), I do apologise to those top-class Ridgebacks and and handlers who have not been mentioned. Our comfort must be that in their true value to a real Ridgeback owner, all Ridgebacks are equally wonderful!

LOUSTIGENS DOUGLAS

This remarkable male lived through not one, but two Swedish and Nordic show careers from the late seventies to the late eighties. Having been away from the ring for some years, he made it back as a veteran and continued to compete successfully with several generations of new Ridgebacks, all the way up to his tenth year. Douglas was less refined than many of today's winners. His head, though with mathematically perfect proportions of 1:1:1, looked heavyish, with slightly loose lips. His coat was medium wheaten, possibly on the lighter side, in comparison with many a show matador of other ages and countries. The ridge was of impeccable length. He also had a little white on his toes on all his paws (some people thought this in fact helped to underscore his movements). However, he exemplified two qualities that can produce true winners.

LouStigens Douglas was a mover that could hardly be surpassed. A well-built dog with an equally well-developed sense of rhythm (yes, just like us human beings, dogs also differ), he just looked so different.

Loustigens Douglas. A systematic winner that does not have the final polish in all details must have something very special: In the case of Douglas, the son of Dalecarlia in the heartland of Sweden, it was front and rear angulation, the absolutely perfect croup, plus a "go" that made him stand out, especially in motion. This dog was used to daily biking exercise up to 20 or more kilometres per day. Just like Champions such as Vumba, Shangara's Checheni or Marsabit M'Fumo, Douglas also produced a high percentage of new winners.

He was also trained into physical almost-perfection, at his prime biking over 12 miles (20 kms) per day. In addition, he had a show presence which could be seen but hardly described. The globally well-known Zimbabwean judge Sammy Wallace put it well; "He was a real character, very special, but I cannot explain how."

One hears many stories about litters in which one, or possibly two puppies stand out, through their behaviour, thanks to their activity level, because of their mischief, or because they are just pampered by their (canine) mothers from the very first day. In a lot of these cases these individuals have gone on to be very successful show dogs. Presence counts for a lot in the show ring, but is hard to breed and hard to describe.

With show dogs, especially those who excel in some extremes, like Douglas in running, then focus on this feature, refine it to perfection. Train the dog to run at a reasonably slow pace. For instance, biking with a dog at a pace, requiring the dog to gallop, will produce negative results, unless the only objective is to increase the physical condition – or cut the dog's nails! A Ridgeback loves high speed and he or

she will show it as soon as possible – not least in a big show ring, when you wanted to move at the trot. Also, you risk developing 'gallop muscles' with more emphasis on the back and upper loins.

Plan your showing upon presenting the strongest points instantly; check where the judge is looking when you enter the ring, and, without obstructing your fellow competitors, see if you can enter from a corner which gives you some running already when you take your position in the line-up.

CAINEABELS RED LOTUS

The CaineAbel bitch that is commonly called Loppis is an example of a modern breeding where care for finish is great, but also where you find the overall correct proportions. The front is strong, yet not too massive; the depth of the chest is good, yet with the correct manageable width. The overall angulation is sound and the feet strong. This successful Swedish bitch, bred and shown by Mrs Ulla Thedin, might be the dark horse among the examples of Great Ridgebacks. Loppis is not exactly an

A long, elegantly curved ribcage creates an overall impression of gracefulness and also denotes significant speed. The bone structure of this bitch, the successful Ch. CaineAbels Red Lotus, is strong yet not heavy and does nothing to distract from the overall feminine touch.

Photo: Ulla Thedin.

unknown soldier, because she has been awarded International and Nordic Champion titles, and carried the Nordic Winner title of 1997. She also won the large Dutch RR Speciality Show, one of the finest on the European continent, in 1998. What is exceptional about this bitch is the consistency of her results as well as the soundness of her temperament. She can sparkle in the ring, and yet she has also proved to have that unique ability to relax during long trips or long shows.

Very seldom do you buy, or even breed a winner. You make a winner. The understanding of and caring for the mental aspects of a young Ridgeback are instrumental, and often decisive, in preparing the dog for future glory. It is no surprise that Mrs Thedin is not only a successful breeder and show handler, but has also invested time and energy in understanding true breed characteristics. If you aspire for consistent top results in breeding, your curiosity and education must be above average!

VUMBA

This exceptional show as well as stud dog became a household name when winning the World title in Valencia in 1992. One of

his strengths lies in a brilliant male head, with an interesting twinkle in the eye, in between sharpness and humour. While, in his prime, he was a good runner, that was not the key to ultimate success. Then, again, his ability to stand up naturally, with equal balance on all four feet, without the handler even needing to touch him, gave him a cutting edge. His contact with the owner and handler Rens Trappel became legendary and many younger handlers have tried to learn this technique of just talking to a dog, holding eye contact in the ring and building his ring presence through just stimulating the dog's natural liveliness and curiosity.

Naturally, by focusing on showing a top-class head to the judge as prominently as possible added to the strength of this real show team. The relaxed showing style and the positive attitude of the dog, which treated every show appearance as a pleasant adventure, meant that Vumba succeeded in shows for an amazing number of years and he, no doubt, goes to the records as the best-known Dutch Ridgeback of the 90s.

No Ridgeback will be a consistent winner unless it likes showing. The difference in performance will then be significantly

The Netherlands have produced many top-winning Ridgebacks over the years. Yet, it is hard to find a comparison to the great Vumba, who started his stardom in the early nineties by winning the World Winner title, then went on to top honours virtually all around Europe. This dog shows masculinity all over, with strong feet carrying a muscular body and a top class head.

Photo: R. van Trappel.

influenced by how the handler can channel this sensation of positive emotions in the ring. Not all individuals have the open mind of a Vumba, making it possible to take his showmanship into extremes. But the contact with your dog can and must be trained. I tend to agree with the saying that when it comes to having the ability for keeping a close contact, your dog has it – but as to the handler, well, some have it, some don't. It is also noteworthy that offspring from Vumba have shown that they have had the same qualities for growing, slowly and surely, in attitude and presence in the ring.

ZURITAMU IMARA

This rather young bitch, judging it from the merit list, has managed to defeat all males twice in the German RRCD annual Top Ten list. This is a tough challenge for any bitch because she tends to have no more than seven to eight months a year of peak condition.

I also tend to view this bitch as another extreme. Her head is cute and feminine, without being a winner. The front is exceptional and the length of body ideal. Her colour is correct yet not eye-catching. The most visible feature is the lightness as well as length of her stride when in motion. No doubt, when comparing a number of Ridgebacks with top-class movements, one still notices extreme ease in the movements. Imara, bred by the Spengler family outside Hamburg, has mostly been shown by a young, naturally talented handler, presenting Imara with that extra lightness (for the lack of a better word) both in motion and when standing up. Combining a running style with a loose leash and a free-standing technique almost without any positioning by hand, the dog has seemed relaxed yet enthusiastic and the judge has, even in static evaluation, been reminded of the dog's pattern in motion.

The more a dog can be given its own 'label' of uniqueness, the better the chance that it stands out, especially in big classes. Just as a dog with a magically superb head can remind the judge of its qualities by, for instance, looking at the judge when in motion, features such as ease

Zuritamu Imara is a long, lean and slender bitch, which should ideally be seen in motion. The strong front is in full harmony with perfect angulation in front and in rear.

Photo courtesy: Roberto.

and elegance in motion can be communicated even when the dog is still. The secret is that the handler has been able to read the dog's qualities well and adjust the handling to suit them. It also goes almost without saying that when showing under tough conditions, like extreme heat (or cold), or in large classes, the dog must be brought to comfort and rest in between the decisive moments in the ring.

RYDGEWAYS AFRICAN HUNTER

The story of Hunter and his keen handler and friend, Mr Marek, of Germany, is almost a fairytale. Mr Marek's first show dog died young and he received Hunter as his new dog. This is one of the many great offspring of the German star Besal Fatoka and a dog with an absolutely stunning male head. This dog has been shown many, many times, with his career divided almost into two halves. In the early days, whether because of tension or because of a deliberate decision, Hunter was shown in short leash, almost strung up. He always stood as a statuette, scoring top points thanks to his head, but he never showed top-quality movement. But, when he already a few years old, the handler and owner changed styles, training the dog to show in free trot, and suddenly the European shows had got a virtually new team. The wonderful enthusiasm and sportsmanship never changed, but the results did. In 1996 the biggest of all the awards Hunter had received by then came in the Hungarian heat – The World Winner title and Best of Breed.

A single feature is seldom enough to make a consistent winner, probably with the exception of individuals that have really excelled in movement. But with good, if not unique, overall qualities and soundly shown movements, the first impression given by a superb head can take you a long way. There are other lessons to be learnt from Hunter as well; you can change showing styles even with an adult dog. And, being a genuinely good winner, as well as, when it happens, being a good loser, pays dividends. Seldom has the Ridgeback audience cheered a World Winner as wholeheartedly as it did Hunter and Mr Marek.

Rydgeway's African Hunter shows what the Ridgeback Standard means by an 'alert' and upstanding dog. This is a Champion with balance in all details.

Photo G. Marek.

MERTEN

The successful son of the great Vumba, Merten, is an example of a Ridgeback that has had a long and even development period. Shown regularly from his early days, the results grew from promising to good to outstanding. Merten has an even better length of body than his father and a very sharp, distinct head, which adds to his presence. He was, in the first years, shown rather hard, and handled somewhat aggressively. Then he grew into the partnership role with his owner and handler, Mr Weinmann from Germany. Merten has also defied a number of common wisdoms, such as that a good mover cannot develop into an excellent mover over time. The mature Merten is a dog that moves far above average. This dog has won big shows, from German

A classic Ridgeback outline, with balanced angulation, excellent length of body and a solid prosternum (chest bone). The German Champion Merten is one of the success stories of the late nineties. This male shows a masculine head, with correct dark eyes, with that hard-to-describe balance between clear masculinity and Ridgeback elegance.

Photo: H-J. Weinmann.

Ravrar Red Cor Caroli:
My personal choice as the ultimate Ridgeback bitch; perfectly balanced, with no traces of weaknesses in front. This head is superbly feminine, yet no-one could find any lack of power. Caroli was a bitch that reached the heights when one found not only soundness and functionality, but also sheer brilliance in small details. Even top-class Ridgebacks usually present more overall soundness than perfection in details; Caroli broke that general rule.

specialities to French and Dutch ones, but he still lacks his well-deserved world titles. Merten is, generally, a big-show dog, with a balance of alertness and endurance that makes him visible throughout several hours of showing.

Even sons and daughters of great winners need to find their own style and their own way of showing. A copy is never as good as the original; but a development, which finds its personal strength, can make the dog surpass the past stars. One challenge of the sensitive balancing act, so well handled by the team of Mr Weinmann and Merten, is to show frequently enough so that the dog and the handler can find each other, while not boring the dog by over-showing too early in life.

RAVVAR RED COR CAROLI

She was an Australian Champion bitch which had it all. Of upper medium size, she combined an exceptional front and neckline with a firm topline and totally balanced angulation. The assessment of this dog can be made by quoting my own comments from the 1989 Speciality in Sydney, where I made Caroli Best of Breed.

"Feminine head with good bite. Good colour of eyes and good ear-setting. Elegant rib cage, correct croup, hocks well let down. Stable and pleasant temperament. An excellent mover, with powerful hind leg movements and parallel movement when viewed coming and going." Femininity all over, yet she had strength in movements that took her to trotting speeds matching those of any top-class male. Possibly the ultimate class act among Ridgeback bitches.

When you get your dream bitch, who is feminine all through, let her develop her physical strength in a natural way. With angulation and mental harmony in place, your bitch will grow into her ultimate shape without any extreme physical training. Training to handle a Ridgeback means learning to control a balanced entity with as little influence as possible, so as not to rock the overall balance. This, self-evidently, does not suggest you should neglect the physical condition of your bitch – just that you should let it develop in a natural way.

SHANGARA'S CHECHENI

This is the all-time star of South African breeding and the pride, among a long list of Champions bred by the Megginson family, of the Shangara lines. Paco, as he was known around the world, was a rather extreme show dog. In fact, he also turned out to be a superb stud dog, and I could have chosen to highlight several of his offspring. However, Paco was special – exceptionally easy to handle on the one hand (I have had the pleasure of showing Paco), with his positive attitude to the show ring and to running, but pretty hard on the other hand, as he had his outstanding side and also his less winning side. Simplifying things, he had a head, neck, front and general presence that made one want to show him as much with his face towards the judge as possible. Paco was also a unique Ridgeback insofar as he not only accepted (reasonable) handling by a stranger, but he gave his own signals to the handler about how to carry out the show!

Both breeding and showing is not always about perfection but about finding and focusing on elements of extreme quality. Positive thinking, and the skills to analyse a dog, make it possible to make stars out of dogs that are on the extreme side, combining outstanding strengths with certain weaknesses (which, under no circumstances, can be read as faults). Paco was a classic example of strength well utilised.

KIJASAMAN DIKIMBA ZURI

This Danish bitch, owned by Inger and Sören Holmgaard, has had a long and truly international career. She is a bitch of upper medium size, with superb length of body, a head with that little magic that can thrill judges and with a show dog temperament that gives her a sparkling visibility. Her career has in many ways been a parallel to the great male in Europe of the mid-1990s, Vishala Kinghunter Lance. Kimba was Best of Opposite Sex with World Winner as well as European Winner titles a number of times during Lance's reign. Kimba is one of the very durable show dogs, which can take long trips (sometimes harder with a bitch than a male), and she has, on her impressive merit list, titles from Berlin to Lisbon. Another of her secrets has been to accept her owner's skilled handling without showing any reaction or irritation in the ring, making it possible to adjust her to perfection standing up in front of the judge.

Ch. Shangara's Checheni had a show presence that only a few, if any, Ridgebacks have matched. This male has also brought additional quality overseas, e.g. in the UK and USA.

Photo B. Carlson.

Kijasaman Dikimba Zuri, a female that basically has it all, from proportions of body to angulation and expression, is the internationally most successful Danish Ridgeback of all times. She has won both World and European Winner titles and has, for years, been a respected name throughout the Continent.

Photo: S. Holmgaard.

If a Ridgeback stands up by him or herself in the ring, great. But this is not to say that a demanding handler/owner might not want to polish the dog's show technique to perfection. It takes skill to handle a dog in the ring, in order not to highlight weaknesses rather than build strengths. Training in front of a mirror, or, in modern times, with a friend taking video shots is a good idea. Kimba has been a good example for many younger enthusiasts in top-class show handing. Winning a few shows is not impossible with a regularly good dog. Winning systematically tells the star from the good dog.

PARIH'S GHALI-M'ZUNGO

This is a Swedish superstar, with ancestors from the US Safari lines on his father's side, while the mother's lines go back to South African Glenaholm material. This background is interesting insofar as one can, and frequently should (assuming the skills are there), go for total outbreeding, where a detailed analysis of the physical features of the parents outweigh the interest in looking at pedigrees. 'Nelson', as he is called by his owner/handler Carina Pergren, is a reasonably tall male, with exceptional length of body and a softness in his movement which makes it look almost amazingly easy to move around the ring. Movement has been one of his strengths. The ability to stand up like a Greek statue for a considerable length of time is another. Nelson has taken no less than four Best-Rhodesian-Ridgeback-in-Sweden titles, possibly Europe's toughest competition,

Parih's Ghali-Mizungo, a show star that has lasted for over half a decade in tough competition. Note the elegant neck and long, elegant ribcage.

Photo: O. Rosenquist, Sweden.

and won big shows all over the Nordic region.

Taking a Ridgeback puppy from an experimental litter takes courage and some self-confidence in selecting puppies. When you are successful, you can end up with a unique show dog, as in the case of Nelson. Above this comes all the hard work to keep a rather large-size runner in top shape, not least during the main show season, the Nordic winter, when snow and cold make outdoor exercise almost impossible. Nelson and Ms Pergren have shown it can be done.

SARULA GUKATIWA
Mrs Linda Costa and Gukatiwa did what every big winner must succeed in doing – picking exactly the right show for an international breakthrough. In this case, the big win (among others, less well-known outside Africa) was timed to perfection, that is, for the 75th Anniversary Show of the Rhodesian Ridgeback Parent Club in Harare, Zimbabwe in 1997. This is a young lady (two at the time of the above mentioned show) which is a deep red, glistering little powerhouse. Not as elegant as some of the great show bitches, but with an overall soundness that makes one wish

one could see this dog at full speed in the African terrain. No surprise that, at a closer look, we find her to be an outstanding example of correct Ridgeback musculature – well-trained, very lean, long and elastic. Good physical condition with well functioning muscles – together with sound angulation – is a trustworthy recipe for healthy movements. Gukatiwa is one of the representatives of the dogs I have chosen to portray, that I hope will stimulate breeders to keep up their ties, in breeding terms, with the home countries of the breed.

A sound Ridgeback is not all about proportions, size or skeletal excellence. The 'software', that is, muscles, must be well developed, but so must the mental side. It is possible to forget that two identically built dogs might not, for instance, move equally well. Individuals with a developed sense of correct movement systematically produce better movement. Gukatiwa is a great example of this fact.

SHADYRIDGE MABRUKI MBILI
This was a top dog, bred by a Swedish lady in the US, which ended up in far-away Finland. Marianne Aaltonen, one of the present-day pioneers of internationalism in

Sarula Gukitawa is superbly balanced with a rather compact, powerful body – yet she is elegantly feminine. Her colour is darkish red, on the upper end of correct coat colours.

Finland's breakthrough in large international circles came thanks to Shadyridge Mabruki Mbili winning the World Winner title in the home country of the International Kennel Club, Belgium. Two words are enough to describe the head – classically masculine.

Photo: M. Aaltonen.

the Finnish Ridgeback world, took good care of the potential this male offered. Bruki, as he was nicknamed, started his steep climb to the very top during the season of 1994-95, crowning it with a World Winner title in Brussels 1995, in the toughest possible environment. The single word to describe this male is elegance. It has been romantically said that the perfect voice of a tenor is like a glittering pearl balancing on the top of a water cascade. To my knowledge there is no equally good description of the ultimate balance in a dog. So you have to settle for noticing that when you strike the right balance between mobility, power and elegance, you know that just one degree in any direction would

have been wrong. Bruki, who passed away far too early, in 1998, will have the honour of symbolising the multitude of top dogs originating in the US. This Champion fulfils the criterion that I had first-hand knowledge of him.

Soft handling of a Ridgeback, and especially a reasonably sizeable male, is neither easy nor common. Shadyridge MaBruki, shown by Ms Aaltonen, was an excellent example of a dog that almost seemed under-handled. Yet he performed at his peak whenever needed. It takes a very special dog and a very special handler to achieve this. The absolute mastery of show handling is when you hardly notice it at all.

KINGHUNTER'S CASSIOPEJA-LIONSTAR

Another bitch that was an extreme rather than an overall star. Pepeja, winning three consecutive Swedish Top Ten victories from 1988-90, had an exceptional head, which has hardly been surpassed and seldom matched. She was small-medium in size, normally a disadvantage when competing with males for Best of Breed. It did not do her any harm. The ridge was correct, not glorious, and the colour was just normal (a rather common problem in colder countries in which dogs develop thicker undercoats and less shine). She won numerous Best in Group placings, and took Best in Show rankings from Sweden and Finland down to sunny San Marino. The secret was simple: she loved showing and even more so, she adored anyone who wanted to approach and touch her. Long, lean muscles and a liking for running freely whenever she was let loose, gave her a better-than-average physical condition. It also paid back when showing at veteran level, which she did

The first undisputed 'girl-power' in the Swedish Ridgeback world was Kinghunter's Cassiopeja-Lionstar, three times Top-Ten winner and also successful on the Continent. Notice the sharpness and classic proportions of the head and the long, lean muscles.

with considerable success until after eight years of age.

The close-to-perfect Ridgeback head, where the 1 to 1 to 1 proportions are correct to the millimetre, is rare. However, if an intense, interested look with dark, penetrating eyes is added, then there is a little touch of magic in the expression. If Ridgebacks with these qualities are shown logically, that is always entering the ring so that the judges first see the expression, it can take the dog a very long way up. It did for Cassiopeja-Lionstar.

MARSABIT M'FUMO

A male hard to describe in one sense – was his greatest performance as a top winning show dog or as a globally acknowledged stud dog? Pauline Sadler and Pat Clancy Worrell, who bred M'Fumo, and Matt and Jan Benson-Lidholm who made him an Australian winner never to be forgotten, have to decide. The Swedish breeder Ann-Mari Hilding recognised his exceptional qualities and so imported his semen, which has shown to be worth gold. Her own breeding from M'Fumo has done fine, and the Aakemba kennels, having being allowed to use the semen, have achieved significant results. M'Fumo's main strengths were in the way he controlled his size which added to the extreme rhythm of his movement. Correct head, good front and a little extra in his stern expression made him the show star. What made him a great sire? Can one ever really know? The most logical theory is that this dog was, in fact, very hard to fault on any point.

The mystery of the excellent stud dog will

Marsabit M'Fumo. Medium size; medium strength in bone; excellent balance between masculinity, strength and elegance in head – combine this with correct angulation and relaxed, easy movements, and you have a Champion. Among details, one can note the superbly strong feet, and the hocks well let down. The qualities of Marsabit M'Fumo have been carried over to new generations.

remain just that. No doubt, an individual with few or no faults, born from parents of homogeneous quality, helps a lot. Still, we do not know if we will get faultless offspring or sparklingly great offspring. Only trying can give the answer. What has been clear, not least thanks to the use of Marsabit M'Fumo on the other side of our globe from his native Western Australia, is that the technique of using frozen semen is a real blessing for small or medium size breeds.

BEARSTAR DIAMOND WILLOW

A single show made this bitch famous, always to be mentioned when looking for breakthrough performances. Born in Australia, she was exported to Sweden where Ms Veronica Gomes-Hansson made her a show dog. In the fall of 1997 Bearstar Diamond Willow was the first Ridgeback ever to win the Group at the Stockholm December show. This is one of the legendary shows in the world, comparable with, if not Wimbledon, at least the Australian or Italian Open in tennis. At the same time the young Rex Ventor kennels became a household name. This Bearstar bitch is, as are so many big winners, of correct body proportions, thus offering long, pace-setting strides. That the big win in Stockholm was no lucky event has later been shown beyond doubt. Diamond Willow proved it, for instance, by winning the Norwegian RR Speciality 1998 (and we should not forget that the 1998 World Winner RR came from Norway).

Ridgeback owners in many countries have long complained that their breed is too small to be recognised in the Group finals, especially in bigger shows. There is naturally a certain truth in this complaint. On the other hand, well shown, top-quality Ridgebacks sooner or later get their breakthrough. The superb results that, for instance, US Ridgebacks have achieved in all-breed shows prove this point. It also requires the handlers to enter the Group rings with a fighting spirit. Bearstar Diamond Willow has made the strong Swedish Ridgeback world a lot stronger by showing what the breed can do in the big rings.

APALACHEE UMQOLO OF PRONKBERG

This is a tall, almost slim male, of dark red coat colour and a majestic elegance when standing still. This South African champion male should not, however, be seen standing still – because when showing he is great, when running he is absolute world-class. Promoted by the legendary Dr Potgieter, bred and shown by Mrs Fitzgerald, this is a male that sets the targets high for anyone

Bearstar Diamond Willow (Sweden). The merits of this bitch speak for themselves, but when one needs to find that single word to describe Bearstar Diamond Willow it would be "energy". It is not uncommon that some dogs systematically do better in Group and Best in Show finals. This takes entity rather than detail, plus sparkling energy and stamina. This well-balanced bitch has proven she has all of the qualities that make an individual stand out among other breeds.

Photo courtesy: Studio Per Unden.

A study of excellence in movement. The South African Ch. Apalache Umqolo of Pronkberg charmed the spectators at the 75th anniversary of the Parent Club, held in Harare, with his typical gait.

who wants to compete in Southern African rings. Umqolo moves with that effective, low, almost grass-licking ease that only perfect angulation can offer. In smaller details, he might not be as refined as some of the world greats, but all of it is compensated for by the soundness of the dog in motion. In the end, the quality of movement is where the greatness of any individual Rhodesian Ridgeback starts or ends.

The debate about the size of Ridgebacks will be eternal. The original Breed Standards, often changed (presumably in many cases because of personal likes or dislikes), are too vague to give clear signals. The useless discussions about weights have further confused the real issue. In the end, function is the checkpoint. Anyone who has seen a male move like Umqolo of Pronkberg must realise that a discussion about slight size variation is futile. Look at how the dog performs.

JANAK MAJA OF MKISHI

Way back, in 1987, this British bitch wrote a little chapter of national RR history. Maja became the first liver-nosed Ridgeback to win a Challenge Certificate. Breeding top class liver-nosed individuals is exceptionally difficult. Maja had superb balance, outstanding angulation and a charming head of correct proportions. Her feet might have carried a little bit too much white, but then, again, she had the light yet warm amber-coloured eyes that are so decisive in a liver-nosed Ridgeback. Furthermore, during a period when English Ridgebacks, with some great exceptions, had some problems with body length, Maja set an example for many a competitor, be it black- or liver-nosed.

In my view the genetics behind liver-nosed Ridgebacks are not yet sufficiently known. It seems likely that it is not only the colour scheme that is different, but it has been, for instance,

A very strong, large-size male, with outstanding proportions in body and strength in front and bone. Ch. Mirengo's Mandambo is one of many from the successful Mirengo lines which all tend to show real power and body length.

Photo courtesy: A. Dixon.

difficult to find liver-nosed dogs with balanced bone structure. Some breeders have made it a matter of priority to produce high-class liver material. Still, you see amazingly few liver Ridgebacks in the statistics of top-winning individuals. Sometimes judges also seem to be reluctant to place a 'different' Ridgeback on the winner's spot. Maja did a lot to change that.

MIRENGO'S MANDAMBO
This was Ann Woodrow's legend from some 20 years back. He was the most extreme of all the superstars covered in this chapter. Large, no doubt. Long in body, powerful to the limits with outstanding angulation all around. The head would not have made him a Champion, but the rest did. His movements were unique in the UK, for his time and his ring presence can only be described as royal. He had a white patch on the chest, the size of a male hand. Why would anyone bother to criticise that, in a superbly sound dog? His movement was amazingly easy for such a powerhouse. In addition to his physical advantages, he had a temperament that made me melt – controlled into his toenails, but arrogantly disinterested in a way that must have been deliberate. He was the classic Ridgeback, accepting strangers but with limited enthusiasm. I could wish that there would one day be an international Hall of Fame, if even only a virtual one. Mandambo would be a must in that distinguished company.

The question of how much deviation from the Breed Standard, for example in weight and height, should be allowed, cannot be exactly answered. The normal position must be 'as little as possible'. Then, again, there are exceptions. They must remain exactly that, but they must also be given credit for all their virtues. The real challenge is to recognise the true exception when you see it – and to avoid making exceptions when there is not enough merit for it.

KALAHARI'S BUBEZI

If Mirengo's Mandambo was an extreme male, so is Kalaharis Bubezi as a female. The proportions are not comparable, because Bubezi cannot be classified as anything but a large medium-sized bitch. But she is strong; she almost borders on being a 'masculine' bitch, with strong bone and very well developed, correct and long muscles. Then, again, she is soundness all over, from the deep black nose to the tip of the tail. In addition, her expression creates excitement, almost magnetism. Bubezi had her real break-through when taking the prestigious Copenhagen Winner title in 1996. The year after, she repeated that performance, plus taking Best of Breed at the European Winner show in Denmark. Bubezi is shown with style, though with an interesting technique, mostly resembling some handling from bigger breeds, by her owner Susan Falck.

Mirengo's Mandambo and young Bubezi are listed after each other, one star from the past, one young and upcoming winner, because they both deserve their titles by having certain qualities in abundance – and making the very best of them. For anyone who thinks it is constructive to look for details to fault in such dogs, I can only comment that a Ridgeback is a matter of entities, not details. The great entity is always a fair distance above the mere sum of good details.

VISHALA KINGHUNTER LANCE

This Australian-bred dog that became a living legend in Europe is a worthy closure to a review of dogs that have had that little bit extra, making them more than mere winners. Lance, about half an inch (1 cm) over the official maximum height, is a long, elegantly bodied male, with correct proportions. He has a correct head, though perhaps not with a memorable expression. The ridge is exceptional, but hardly the reason for all his successes. He was bred by

In 1997, the bitch Kalahari's Bubezi, became the first Nordic-born Ridgeback to win the FCI-European Winner title (the legendary Lance was born in Sydney). This is a bitch with an intense expression and an overall balance, which produces consistently good show results.

Photo: Joergen Bak Rasmussen.

The all-time most successful Ridgeback to fly the Swedish colours (despite Australian origins), Vishala Kinghunter Lance. Notice the power in the muscles and the exceptional length of body, as well as the all-out balance in angulation, which together formed the foundation of the winning movements of this male.

Photo courtesy: Rosy Brook-Risse.

Mrs Bacon and Mrs Hawkins, in Sydney, from two top-class dogs. They were taking a chance, as his parents were pretty dissimilar in type. Movement has been Lance's trump card, and is best described as dancing. He always liked showing and he, like so many other big winners, is self-assured enough to make aggressive gestures unnecessary. He started his career as a junior in places around Europe where neither he nor his owner had ever been seen in a show before. He took one World Winner title (in 1994) and three European titles and added twelve National Championships. When he ended his career, winning the Veteran class at the Helsinki World Show in 1998, he was universally adored. That reputation he built by sparkling in the ring – hardly extreme, but definitely different, with a physical presence that few have been able to match.

Both Lance's parents were show dogs. Yet they were very different and Lance was another of the daring combinations that just paid off. His full brother won the 1997 Melbourne show in connection with the World Congress, with some 240 competitors. The good fortune might have been in the fact that the breeding was based upon top marks for movement in the parents. We can assume that sticking to lines that systematically produce good movers is a sound starting point. Lance has given almost similar qualities to his progeny and the future will show how long these qualities are carried along.

9 BREEDING RIDGEBACKS

After studying basic genetics and realising that you will have to face the challenge of the mating, the birth of the litter and the rearing and feeding of the puppies, you have to make the ultimate, crucial decision – choosing a breeding partner. Good breeding is not done by magic; it is hard work, and you will need logic and some luck. You need to plan the mating, starting from the analysis we have already discussed, that is, knowing the strengths and the weaknesses of your Ridgeback. In addition you need to be aware that some of the qualities that your dog might lack – for good or ill – compared to its parents or litter brothers and sisters, could show up in the next generation.

ASSESSING THE BREEDING PAIR
A thorough study of potential partners is essential. If you are using your Ridgeback for the first time, try to find an experienced mate. Then back to the drawing-board. What do you know about the parents of the proposed partners? Use a pen and paper. Below is the so-called PeCa scheme, a grid intended to help you form a visual picture of similarities and discrepancies in the

Planning a successful breeding programme takes time and thought – and a degree of luck!

Photo: T. Torkelsen, Norway.

intended parents. The name of the this grid comes from an attempt by the successful Swedish breeder, Stig Petterson and me to assist new breeders in putting their facts which they have researched into some system, hence PeCa. It uses a list of essential qualities. Then it is up to the potential breeder to be able to make a correct assessment of strengths on the proposed 5-point scale, 5 being the top score.

THE ROLE OF NATURE

Breeding is a dialogue with Nature, where Nature holds ninety-nine per cent of the cards and shows only a few of them. The possibilities of variations in any combination are mind-boggling. Simple truths, which have been stated before in this book, include the fact that the best guide to the likely outcome comes by having a very thorough search for data on

QUALITIES	Planned Sire					Planned Dam				
	1	2	3	4	5	5	4	3	2	1
Overall proportions					X	X				
Head:										
Gender typical					•	•				
Proportions 1:1:1				•		•				
Eye colour				•		•				
Teeth & Bite					•		•			
Front					X	X				
Bone					X	X				
Angulation:										
Front angulation					•	•				
Hind angulation					•	•				
Hocks well down					•	•				
Feet				X		X				
Chest:										
Depth of chest					•	•				
Balanced width of chest					•	•				
Length of chest					•	•				
Colour					X		X			
Ridge:										
Length					•	•				
Symmetry of crowns					•	•				
Symmetry of arch					•		•			
Movements					X	X				
Temperament					X	X				

the parents themselves, their litters if they have already produced progeny, and also the grandparents. A common misconception is that a mating produces some kind of compromise, or average, between the parent dogs. Wrong! And here comes the problem with mother Nature: certain individuals and strains clearly have strong tendencies to produce certain features, and these also come through strongly in combinations with different-looking mates. For instance, I have seen problems with the front angulation, from a single side in a breeding, follow through to ten generations. Another factor to take into account is that qualities lost, such as the agility and original behaviour, are lost forever in those strains. Your only solution then is to go for a multi-generation plan using outbreeding – non-related individuals which are presumed to have preserved the qualities lost in the other lines.

It should go without saying that the breeding plan must take into account the Codes of Ethics of the national Kennel Club, as well as the country's Ridgeback club.

The attitude we wish to see in breeding planning is a *positive* search for qualities. This does not mean that one should deliberately neglect faults, but that *fault avoidance is not the target, just a pre-condition*. The idea of planned breeding is to search for strength, to aspire to top quality.

To go back to the above grid, the more top scores (5) you see in points you consider important for your breeding, the better are the chances for a good result. Again, however, you have to remember that the Ridgeback is a mixed breed and

that we have to expect some variations, even within the same litters.

TEN RULES FOR BREEDERS

When you first consider having a litter from your bitch, you must also reflect on what it means to become a breeder. When it comes to responsibility, there is no difference between planning to have a single litter from your pet Ridgeback, or being – or dreaming about being – a large-scale breeder having several fertile bitches of breeding age.

Every litter, every puppy born, brings the breed forward – or if things go wrong, it takes the future of our breed in a negative direction. Hence deciding to breed is deciding a lot more than just mating a bitch. Breeding is not just an undertaking but rather, to borrow the definition of the expert Swedish breeder Bitte Lind, "breeding is a way of life." Below is a list of ten decisive aspects of breeding – we have avoided the worn-out term 'Ten Commandments'.

i. Keep the well-being of the dogs separate from your own life.
The decision to own a dog means accepting responsibility for a companion that is dependent on you for fair treatment in all situations in life. Breeding, with the hard work and day-and-night duties it brings with it, assumes that the breeder knows she or he can live two different lives at once. Your own life, as we all know, includes ups and downs: problems with your work, your personal relationships, your sports, your finances etc. must never have a negative influence on your treatment of your dogs. This prerequisite is even more obvious when you think about a litter at its most

sensitive age, the socialisation phase of its development. It is essential that the entire family stand behind the decision to go into breeding. Rearing a litter is more than one person's duty.

ii. Sort out the economics of breeding.
I assume that because you are already considering buying a dog, this means that you are aware of the economic aspects of dog ownership. Deciding to breed adds a new dimension to this reality. Let us have a basic overview of costs, from purchasing a bitch to having the first litter.

There is the purchase cost of the bitch and then maintaining her, including food, veterinary costs, kennel and breed club membership fees, annual vaccination costs, X-raying for hip and elbow soundness, and insurance.

Then there is the cost of obtaining merits for your dog (in some countries this starts with a mandatory passing of exterior tests, possibly also temperament tests); entry fees to dog shows, car costs and, perhaps, overnight stops at hotels, and your own food expenses have to be included.

Looking for a suitable male for your bitch, which normally means additional travel, either to shows or to dog owners, costs money. When the mating is decided, there are the costs of travelling to and from the home of the male (yes, girl always comes to boy in the dog world), plus phone and other communication expenses.

There are possible vet costs to check when the right moment for mating is there. After the cost mating itself, there are additional food costs for the pregnant bitch, and, presumably, also an ultrasound check by the vet to confirm the pregnancy.

You need to build a kennel, or at least prepare a sound whelping and puppy room in your home, stock up the essential utensils for the whelping, and to buy food for the litter as the puppies grow.

Possibly, though we hope not, there may be vet costs related to birth complications. When the litter is born, you will need to vaccinate the puppies, get the necessary vet certificates, register the puppies with your national Kennel Club, handle the de-worming, get the IDs for each pup, and possibly spend some money on advertising the litter. Put some reserve money in a special bank account. On the one hand – and we will discuss this below – you should plan for a sound follow-up to your litter by planning for ongoing relations with the buyers. On the other hand, the product liability legislation in all advanced societies makes you responsible for possible hereditary problems that might occur.

iii. Keep in touch with the puppy buyers.
It is not enough that you deliver a sound puppy, with all vaccinations and documents in order, to the new family. One also assumes that you have handed over a "pet-owner's guide" in some form, including detailed advice for feeding the pup. Many experienced breeders plan their follow-up in a systematic way, including mailing small "kennel bulletins" to the pup buyers from time to time. Building a team spirit has more advantages than just creating a new, bigger circle of friends. In case the ownership goes sour with the buyers, you also have a much-increased likelihood of being able to handle the re-placing of the dog, or buying it back. Note that not all legislation accepts a clause in a contract

Breeding is wonderful when you have made the full commitment, done your homework and got your litter. Though, this level of contentment should not be expected to last too long. A litter of Ridgeback are small angels which have tremendous bouts of energy.
Picture courtesy: S. Clayborough.

which stipulates that the breeder always has the first choice to buy back a dog if the new owners run into problems. Remember that, for instance, divorces happen more frequently than we would like to think; children can develop allergies; people can lose their jobs and the financial ability to own and care for pets.

My wife and I have sold puppies with a first dog-show entry fee included in the price. If you hope for the offspring to be seen in the show ring, this is a practical solution.

iv. Avoid being a large-scale commercial breeder.

Building a proper kennel near to your home is essential. You do want to be a good breeder with close contacts with your dog or dogs, but you should not be a prisoner to the realities of dog ownership or breeding.

No one who is interested in human/dog relationships would even think about building a puppy factory. Unfortunately these exist, and in Belgium, for instance, the home country of the international Kennel Club, the FCI, these dog factories can also send their offspring to gigantic animal supermarkets, from which the poor animals are sold (in the best-case scenario) without much control of how and to whom. The reason why these animal supermarkets exist is less that buyers are uneducated – this is a fact of life – but rather as the result of the existence of immoral dog breeders. These people exist in all breeds, but as soon as a breed increases in popularity, it is in special danger. Ridgebacks are, in many countries, getting into this danger zone of over-popularity.

v. Have the heart and resources to care for the ageing dogs.

When your bitch, or bitches, have produced some litters and you have had the pleasure of seeing new, lovely Ridgebacks born to this world, please remember all that the bitches have given you. Give them a worthy life, all possible companionship and good care after they have passed the limit of the fertile age. Technically, bitches are fertile well into maturity but no responsible breeder would think of breeding from a veteran bitch. Many Ridgeback clubs nowadays regulate the numbers of litters, as well as breeding ages. The same thing, by the way, should be the case with show dogs.

Once a ring career is over, do not thank your wonderful campaigner by just selling off the dog, or leaving her or him with a minimum of care in an impersonal environment.

vi. Accept turning into a human cleaning machine.
The less visible reality of dog breeding is the need for absolute hygiene. Please accept that life as a breeder is unromantic on a very regular basis. Puppies are exceptionally sensitive and are exposed to all sorts of risks early in their lives. The best life insurance for your puppies, even more than the early vaccinations, is cleanliness.

vii. Screen prospective buyers.
Remember how tough the interviews (hopefully) were when you started to ask around for a Ridgeback! Pay the same respect to your puppies. Interview every single potential buyer. Learn to read between the lines. Is the family sound? Do they have small children they worry too much about? How and where do they live? Do they make good contact with your adult dog(s)?

Learn the technique of never promising anything on the first visit of a speculative buyer. Keep a list of all people you have seen and make a systematic choice in the end.

Make sure you can hear what is not said, besides hearing what is told to you. You should naturally have guarantees that the puppy, even as an adult dog, will never be left alone at home for long periods. The absolute maximum a dog can be left is three to four hours per day. Naturally you will not buy arguments such as "the kids will take him out when they are back from school," or "I will go home over the lunch-hour."

viii. Be candid with the potential buyers.
Over the years, I have encountered even serious breeders complaining when articles or books have revealed that Ridgebacks have their own agendas. They can dig themselves out from (almost) any kennel. They demand a lot of physical exercise. They have minds of their own and they are physically strong. Their mentality is that of a very natural dog. In short, a Ridgeback, as I have said before, might not be an ideal 'beginner's dog'. It is wrong for breeders to object to such information being revealed. There is no such thing as over-information. The sheer idea that a puppy seller would not inform potential buyers, to the best of her or his knowledge, about the breed, should be absurd.

The very basis of good dog breeding is honesty and transparency. If there is a puppy in the litter with offset crowns, or a Dermoid Sinus case, or if there are ridgeless puppies, the conscientious breeder informs buyers about this openly. Openness is a hallmark of a good breeder!

It also goes without saying that you should not sell puppies with obvious faults as anything other then pets, and the buyers should be very well aware of this – ideally it should be specified in the purchase contract. I have always favoured the system whereby a Kennel Club allows breeders to register puppies, at the same time getting a special marking in the pedigree barring certain dogs from being used for breeding purposes. The American Kennel Club's 'B' registration is a good example of this. Thus you get the best of two worlds – the Kennel Club gets full data about all litters in its computer systems so that fault detection programmes can be credible, and at the same time you stop incorrect specimens from being used, at least in the official breeding programme.

ix. Build and keep a facts-bank.
One of many reasons to keep in touch with puppy buyers is that the breeder will get feedback. It is essential to learn about how the puppies developed. Which ones, in the end, had the right proportions, the correct length of body, good angulation, etc.? How did they develop mentally? And so on. Build you own 'real-life pedigree'. A normal pedigree is very much a piece of paper, and many a serious breeder has never understood the fascination of looking at pedigrees for hours. Pedigrees become properly informative when you can put facts and details behind them.

Building a facts-bank about your own breeding is only part of the intelligence-gathering which a keen breeder should be doing. When going to dog shows, use a small dictating machine, or take notes, and take plenty of pictures. These, together with information which your club and your colleagues are, hopefully, providing about their dogs will, in the end, help you build a valuable facts-bank for long-term planning of your future breeding.

x. Accept you are a public figure – be a role model!
Once you have started on the path of producing new Ridgebacks, you are an example to the next generation. Be generous, respond to questions and talk to

people who are interested in our breed. Do not stop showing your top-class bitch or your ageing Champion too soon. The market needs examples.

And be an example with your own conduct. Be a sportsman in the ring, be open and honest in your breeding, and be a keen promoter of our breed wherever you are. If you are involved with dog club activities, and, of course, every time your Ridgeback sets foot in a show ring, be an ambassador for the breed in the eyes of dog lovers everywhere.

GETTING STARTED
We now assume that you have dealt with the three absolute musts when making your decision to breed Ridgebacks – or at least to have a first litter. These are:

1 You have read about the breed and formed your own view on the most important qualities required in a good Ridgeback; you have analysed and assessed your own bitch; you have followed the Ethical Codes of your country; you have found some alternative males for her and you are convinced this mating will move the breed forward.
2. You have the time, facilities and financial resources to handle the mating, the whelping and the upbringing of the puppies.
3. You do this out of love for Ridgebacks, not for money!

AGE AND EXPERIENCE
A bitch comes into heat for the first time at around nine to twelve months, though the process can take up to two years without it being deemed unnatural. It should be an

absolute principle never to mate a bitch during her first season. All in all, a bitch should get no more than four, and in very special cases up to five, litters in her lifetime. The final decision should be dependent on her physical condition and also on the sizes of the litters she has borne. The total number of puppies she has given birth to must, in the end, be seen as the decisive factor when assessing how much strain the bitch has been facing. You could say that if the total number of puppies born has not exceeded about 20 in four litters, and a vet gives the green light, you could consider a fifth and final litter.

Do not to use artificial insemination for the first mating. It is also wise to choose a male which has mated bitches before, and the progeny of which can already be assessed.

Males normally become fertile between nine to eleven months of age, some as early as six or seven months. It is totally unfair to use a male who is still in his developmental stage for mating. This can cause irreparable damage to the bones as well as to ligaments. In addition, a male under two years, even if the hip X-rays are good, cannot be said to have been finally cleared as to his hip status. New commercially marketed hip dysplasia X-raying methods suggest that one could lower the minimum age for X-raying. However, there is still not enough statistical evidence to establish that this is foolproof. Finally, thinking about the practicalities of the mating process itself, a first-time bitch is better served by having a steady, experienced partner.

PUPPY DEMAND

We have established that no ethical breeding decision should be based upon economic calculations – other than possibly abstaining – because in the end the total adventure, with vet costs and all the insurance and other expenses, can be a financial burden to the breeder. To be sensible, you also need to check with your national breed club, which, in most countries, will have statistics about the availability of, and the demand for, Ridgebacks. It is the responsibility of the breeder-to-be to ensure that the likelihood of finding not merely buyers, but also good buyers for the puppies, is realistic.

Let us also kill an old myth. There is absolutely no evidence that the bitch will be healthier if she has a litter. Having, or not having, a litter from a bitch makes no difference to her happiness or well-being.

BREEDING CONDITION

It goes without saying that the female has to be in top condition when being mated and when whelping and rearing her puppies. Seasoned breeders have a clear principle: There is a single period when a bitch needs to be kept in excellent physical condition – and that is always! Make sure you exercise your bitch properly, through long walks or by whatever methods you have chosen, and particularly during the weeks leading up to the expected season. However, physically and mentally demanding sports such as lure coursing can cause some stress, which can postpone the coming into season.

Male infertility can be caused by many reasons, one of which is lack of physical condition. If you also own the male, make sure he gets the same good physical training as your bitch. If your male shows a tendency to have fertility problems, turn to an expert clinic. They can perform wonders. In case it is necessary to get frozen semen from your male, make sure you use a first-class clinic. The difference in litter sizes can be staggering.

NUTRITION

First we need an overall view of the nutritional needs of the bitch. For the sake of ease as well as security, we assume that you have chosen to use a high-quality, complete, commercial dog-food brand which, I believe, must be free of additives and colouring agents. Do not add vitamins or calcium to this food. It might upset the scientifically balanced composition of the product.

Before the mating, give the bitch her normal food and do not allow her to become overweight. Most bitches lose their appetite for a while three to five weeks after the mating. This is normal. Some bitches, on the other hand, develop an unnatural appetite. Beware of overfeeding the bitch, as this, among its negative effects, leaves too little room for the puppies to grow. As to securing a sound level of Folic Acid for the bitch ahead of the mating (not the whelping) see Chapter Ten.

Up to week five or six after the mating, depending on the size of the coming litter, the puppies grow slowly and there is no need to feed the bitch any other nutrition than regular maintenance food.

During the last three weeks before the birth of the puppies the mother needs $1^1/2$ times her normal energy. In order to give this additional energy, while at the same time avoiding filling her stomach with too much substance, move her on to puppy food.

During the first 24 hours after the whelping the mother will only need ample amounts of water, plus liquid nutrition such as beef broth. With a small to medium-size litter it can be sufficient to continue with puppy food for the first three weeks. If you have a normal-size litter – six or more puppies – by day 21 after whelping move over to high-energy (heavy-duty) dog food, and keep this going for some two weeks.

As for puppy food, let us discuss this after we have dealt with whelping. But, before we move back to the mating itself, let us finish the comments about the nutritional needs of the female, by reminding ourselves of the need for building in her a sound store of vitamins, minerals and amino acids. If this is not done, there is a high risk of some puppies dying during the gestation period.

THE MATING

The human resources needed for breeding include two people for the mating itself and, ideally, two people for the whelping, one of whom should have experience in checking for Dermoid Sinus. You should also be able to guarantee that the mother will never be left alone for any significant period of time until the puppies are delivered to their new owners a minimum of eight weeks after the birth of the litter.

It is up to the breeder to use one of the available methods for determining when it is the right moment for the first mating. The traditional method is to trust the male. The scientific option is to ask for expert veterinary tests. An experienced male will behave with indifference until the right moment has arrived. Most breeds come into season twice a year, with intervals from

26 weeks or longer. Basenjis, and, interestingly, also some Ridgebacks, come into season only once per year. The pre-season period normally lasts one to two weeks, but can, in extreme cases, be as long as 30 days. During this period the bitch will still fend off any close inspection by males. The bitch drinks and urinates a lot during this time and she can show signs of irritation, even teen-age behaviour.

Make sure that you can get in touch with the owner of the male when you have reason to believe that the bitch is close to time.

Choose a secluded, quiet location for the mating. This is out of courtesy to your dogs – and, sometimes, also to your neighbours, who might not be all that used to Mother Nature's realities. In some cases, the male will just check the bitch by putting a paw and his nose on her back and then, having noticed no resistance, he will be ready to mount her. Sometimes a young bitch needs more courting, so do not be surprised if the couple run around in cheerful play. This is natural. It is also why a fenced-in location should be chosen.

Once the mating has started, you might have to face the fact that the dogs are hanging together for up to 20 minutes (or, on rare occasions, even longer). It is essential that they be kept under control so that the bitch does not suddenly try to run away, thus risking serious damage to both partners. Always use collars on the dogs and have your leashes available. I would also suggest two small chairs for the human assistants!

PREPARING FOR THE WHELPING
Is the bitch carrying puppies? Normal signs

are: that males continue to be interested in her after the end of her season; that her vulva remains somewhat swollen; that she might feel sick between weeks three and five after the mating; that her preparations for breast milk production start around five weeks – which is also when you should see some growth in the size of her stomach; and that by seven weeks you should feel some movements of the unborn puppies. Ultrasound tests can be made to determine the success of the mating after about 25 days, while X-rays can be used from six weeks onwards.

Large breeds normally have a gestation time of 63 days, but be prepared – the big day could come a bit earlier. So start preparations in time. You will need a room for the bitch, in which you can have a puppy box. There should be sufficient daylight, because learning the rhythms of day and night is very important. You must make sure that there is no way that the fast-growing puppies can get to electric cords, or other dangers. For your own comfort there must be an exit through which the mother can go in and out during the first weeks, and with all of her enlarged family after about a month. Carrying puppies out from, and back into, the puppy box a number of times a day soon turns into a very tough routine.

When you plan your space for the mother and her litter, ensure that no cold winds can sweep in across the floor chilling the puppies. Build the area so that you help the mother find a private space when she needs to rest alone during the first two to three weeks. Either you can provide peace for the mother in a part of the box separated by a low fence, or you can place the mother's bed some 8 ins (20 cms) above the main puppy floor. Also make very sure that the mother's water and food bowls are out of reach of the puppies, so they cannot, under any circumstances, be at risk of drowning in the water bowl once they start moving around.

It is an absolute must that you can control the temperature of the environment where the puppies will spend the first two months of their lives. It should be around 90 degrees Fahrenheit (30C) for the first week, around 80-85F (26C) for the next two weeks, and 76-80F (23C) for the fourth and fifth weeks – and remember that the mother's body temperature naturally adds to the heat.

I hope that you have someone with you who is experienced, if this is the first whelping you attend. Prepare a set of potentially necessary items. But, first of all, check and agree on the availability of your nearest, trusted vet and have the phone number at hand. Things do not go wrong all that frequently with a natural breed such as a Ridgeback: these preparations are not for normal occasions but for emergencies.

The regular preparations should include:

• Vetbed, or something similar, with clean spares to offer the mother as soon as her labour is over.
• A huge pile of newspapers, which will be your artificial ground for the puppy room for weeks to come.
• Antiseptic towels (non-alcoholic) and cleansing agents.
• Scissors to cut the cords if necessary (sterilised).
• Clean string for tying cords if that is needed.
• Clean cold drinking water for the mother. (I always go for bottled water, both for the mother and her offspring.)
• A hot-water bottle, kept at a warm temperature.
• Plastic bags in which to put the debris.
• Ready-made, lukewarm beef bouillon for the bitch.
• A note pad and a pen to record the weights of the puppies.
• Weighing scales and a thermometer.
• In reserve keep ready some Dextrose (high energy sugar) in case a puppy needs early extra strengthening.

In larger dog breeds the temperature of the bitch will drop to about 99F (37C) possibly even slightly lower, when the whelping is imminent. The pre-birth stage, with milder pains and cramps, can last a maximum of 10 to 12 hours. If the bitch shows signs of tiredness, or there is no intensification in the contractions, call the vet.

The actual whelping stage, with increasingly heavy pains and contractions, should not drag out for more than one-and-a-half to three hours. If by then the whelping has not started, or the cramps continue irregularly, get a vet. Also, if there are heavy pains and cramps but no birth, this can be caused by, for instance, a misplaced pup – you should get the vet's assistance within the next 30 minutes.

Normally the puppies are born at intervals ranging from five minutes to about one hour. The total whelping procedure should not exceed 12 hours. Usually the bitch changes her behaviour, being more relaxed and paying full attention to the litter, when the last puppy has been born. You might check that there is no puppy left by feeling under the rear part of the stomach.

THE NEW-BORN LITTER

You should record the birth weights of all the puppies, and also take careful note of the "IDs" of each and every puppy. Also, take your time; let the mother settle down, then check to make sure that the puppies quickly develop their own ability to seek the teats and feed themselves.

A healthy newborn litter eats a lot, sleeps well and is reasonably quiet. If the puppies show early signs of discomfort, sleep less and move around, the reason often is insufficient nutrition. Increase the amount of puppy food (commercial dry food) you give to the bitch. Also make sure she has a chance to drink sufficient amounts of water. If the bitch systematically rejects a particular puppy, take it instantly to the vet.

Chances are that this is not a sound individual and, if that is the case, having been checked by the vet it needs to be put to sleep as soon and as painlessly as only a vet can do. If a puppy seems too weak to get sufficient milk from its mother, give it a lukewarm water-and-Dextrose mixture as soon as possible. The chances are this will give the puppy enough energy to start functioning normally.

The ideal is always to avoid artificial feeding. If you face a serious problem, such as an oversized litter or a bitch getting seriously ill, you will have to feed the puppies with baby bottles. Feed them so that you can feel the round shape of a well-fed tummy by stroking the belly of the pup with your finger, slightly above the ribs. Feed them six times a day in the beginning, but avoid feeding them during the night. Use a tested milk-substitute, either

A healthy, problem-free litter is what we all dream about.

Photo: H. Tandefelt.

commercial or home-made. The recipe below is reliable:

Cow's milk (3% fat)	800 ml
Demi-cream (12% fat)	200 ml
Bone meal	6 grams
Citric acid	4 g
1 egg yolk	15 g
Vitamin A	2000 IU
Vitamin D	500 IU

The energy value of this product is approximately 88 Kcal. The milk substitute requirement, measured in grams per 100 grams of body weight of the puppy, is:

1st week	22
2nd week	25
3rd week	28
4th week	30

The normal development of the puppy is that eyes open after 10 to 14 days and ears open after 13 to 17 days. The puppies start recognising the immediate environment by 21 to 28 days. Reactions to sounds and visual impacts occur by three weeks and continue. Teeth begin to develop soon after 21 days – and beware, they grow fast – and the puppies start standing up after three weeks and moving around on all four legs after four weeks.

Do not forget to check the puppies for Dermoid Sinus and repeat this check, on a weekly basis, at least three or four times.

The ridges, as to symmetry, length in proportion to body length, as well as the number and symmetry of the crowns, are clearly visible just hours after birth. By about one week the ridges get blurred for a while. However, it is possible to know almost immediately what the ridge quality of the puppies is going to be. Also, a ridgeless puppy is a ridgeless puppy. This, in my strong opinion, does not alter an otherwise healthy puppy's right to live.

The first period of the litter's development, the neonatal phase, which lasts until the eyes open, demands good-quality food for, and through, the mother, rest and peace, and sufficient warmth as well as hygiene. The transitional phase is after the puppies' eyes open until they start becoming socially aware, that is until approximately three weeks of age. During this phase you need to check that all puppies are getting sufficient nutrition and that one or two weaker individuals do not get pushed to one side by their stronger brothers and sisters. The social awareness dawn is from about three weeks until the end of weaning. This is when it is essential that the puppies not only have contact with their mother, but also frequently with human beings.

Following the end of the weaning, it is also essential – though often forgotten and sometimes hard to arrange – that the puppies can meet their father. He will sometimes be a firm and rough father, but the lessons learnt are lessons for life for the puppies.

If your bitch vomits some of her food into the puppy box, do not get upset or worried. It is natural that the mother feeds the puppies, once the weaning is coming to its end, by "carrying home food to the nest". (It can happen that even the father "brings home food" in this manner!) When the litter grows old enough to eat part of their meals from their own bowls, remember that puppy water and food bowls can be traps. For instance, make sure the water in their bowls is too low for any pup to drown in them, even if a puppy falls asleep with its head on the edge.

Feeding growing litters, today, is easy. Just avoid making things too difficult. Use commercial high-class petfood and follow the instructions without adding too much, or, in fact, anything. However, one trick possibly worth remembering from old hands is that there is a way of teaching the puppies to eat solid food. As soon as the puppies can stand up and start drinking and eating by themselves, while the mother still offers sufficient milk, try a weaning diet as an addition. A combination of good, pure mashed chopped meat in regular maize-soup is very effective.

To conclude this part, a rough indication of the daily nutritional need of a Ridgeback (assuming a bitch will end up at somewhere over 30 kilograms and males, in real life, at or above 40 kilograms) is as follows: (*See chart below*)

HEALTH-CARE AND VACCINATIONS
The bitch offers the puppies significant protection during the breast-feeding

period. It is reasonable to give the litter a first Parvovirus injection soon after the weaning, and no later than one week before sending them to their new homes – a minimum of eight weeks after birth – and again four weeks after arrival in their new homes. Following this, re-vaccination is recommended on a regular yearly basis.

Distemper and Hepatitis vaccinations should normally be given one week before delivery of the puppies to their new owners, at approximately seven or eight weeks, with a re-vaccination four to five weeks after the first shots.

In some countries the puppies also need to be given a Leptospirosis inoculation, as well as Rabies protection. As the medical situations vary between countries, you should ask for expert advice from your vet.

De-worming should take place during the third week after birth and be repeated 10 to 14 days later. Puppies that live in a kennel environment should get a de-worming treatment every 14 days until delivery to their new owners.

The puppies should also have their ID-marking in the ear, or using modern electronic techniques such as a microchip – before they are delivered to their new owners.

Weight of puppy/youngster in kilograms/body weight:

3kg	6kg	12kg	18kg	30kg

Daily nutritional need counted in Kcal per kilogram of body weight:

180-195	145-155	100-115	80-85	60-65

10 HEALTH AND BREED SPECIFIC GENETIC ISSUES

The two musts in any discussion about health and genetic concerns for owners of Ridgebacks are ridge/ridgelessness, and Dermoid Sinus.

THE RIDGE

The ridge, the symmetric hair formation on the back of the Ridgeback, stems from the mane-like formation found in the indigenous African dogs which, mixed with numerous other dog types, eventually formed the present-day Ridgeback. We do know that today's ridge is elegant and almost mathematically symmetrical, which was not the case some 70 years ago. The exact genetic definition of the ridge, as we see it today, is not fully researched. What we do know is that the ridge is carried forward as a dominant genetic quality. After that, we can only speculate about Nature's own definition of what the ridge is composed of.

The origin must have been a mutation. Mutations, as we have been taught, are random changes, though modern science in all its complexity is starting to lean towards the thought that mutations can be 'functionally steered'. I have, for other purposes, discussed mutations and evolution with top-level experts. These are the areas where, as one person told me, the borderlines between science and theology start becoming confused.

It is known for a fact that canine species, in nature and by pressure from a new environment, can change into a new, well-adapted form in 23 to 24 generations. We also know that hair formations exist on canines other than Ridgebacks, for instance the South American mane wolf. One theory is that these hair formations work as part of the animal's signal system, or that it makes them look more formidable. Whether this was a reason for the very early mutation behind the ridge, we will never find out. But we might one day know how ridge ownership versus ridgelessness, in more precise detail, is defined genetically.

The likelihood is that it is the change of growth direction of the hair that is the defining factor. Does it have to be related to the back? Logically I would guess yes, as the area above the spine is where the hair directions are turning left versus right on all dogs. Are the crowns involved? We cannot prove this, and the more likely answer is no.

How today's 'show ridge' is inherited becomes puzzling when we realise how symmetrically faulty ridges can be produced. The most common ridge fault, in show terms – offset crowns – is, in fact, the least interesting; the fact that ridges seem to be 'built in parts' is amazing. We can see complete upside-down arches with two additional crowns; we can see a half arch with an extra crown on one side, in addition to a correct ridge below. We can also see half ridges, i.e. only a left or right side, with one crown and half an arch. Recently, I met a Ridgeback puppy with an extra arch and two crowns in a 90 degree angle to the normal, main ridge. This is an area where we must welcome further studies, perhaps starting from understanding how breeding from faulty ridges turns out. I am not advocating test breeding, but I know for a fact that dogs with, for example, extra crowns, have been used in breeding. Step one would be to monitor the progeny to see if, as one option, there are more faulty ridges than average and for how many generations this would carry on. It would also be interesting so see if the 'parts' theory could be verified statistically.

The basics of genetics is that all qualities are steered by a pair of genes. These genes can be symmetrical, called homozygous, or different, called heterozygous. In our case, talking about ridges, the alternatives are two genes for ridge, or one for ridge and one signalling ridgelessness. Let us call the former (R) and the latter (rl). The capital (R) stands for the fact that the quality for ridge is dominant; i.e. in a heterozygous, or mixed, gene pair this quality over-rides the gene against ridge.

Logically, each offspring gets its gene pair from its parents. Let us look at how the basic quality of carrying a ridge might be transferred from parents to offspring. Before we look at the schemes, there is one caveat: the statistical proportions are valid only when a large number of puppies are born. Where statistical probability says 'half of puppies are ridgeless' this does not, in real life, mean exactly fifty per cent. Were this poor mother to have hundreds of puppies in this combination, the final outcome would get closer to fifty per cent.

Option A:

		Parent A	
		R	R
Parent B	R	RR	RR
	R	RR	RR

This is the ideal situation in modern Ridgeback breeding. Both parents are homozygous for ridge, and all offspring will carry ridges. In addition, all of the offspring will carry the dominant quality for carrying ridges.

Note that the only way to know if the parent is homozygous is to have all the facts about both of *its* parents, which means, for instance, knowing that the parent individual has been mated with another Ridgeback known, for a fact, to carry a gene for ridgelessness and producing only ridged puppies.

Option B:

		Parent A	
		R	rl
Parent	R	RR	Rrl
B	R	RR	Rrl

(Looking back at the comments under Option A, this could, in theory, have been the test mating that gave proof that a certain male or female carries the homozygous qualities for ridge.)

In Option B one of the parents is homozygous, while the other one is heterozygous, that is carries one gene for ridge and one for lack of ridge. The outcome is that all offspring will carry ridges. On the other hand, without this being detected (unless test matings are made), on average fifty per cent of the puppies carry the quality for ridgelessness.

Option C:

		Parent A	
		R	rl
Parent	R	RR	Rrl
B	rl	Rrl	rlrl

Now we have the first combination which produces some puppies which do not carry a ridge. Three quarters, on average, of the offspring carry ridges (though only a third of the puppies with a ridge are homozygous for ridge); fifty per cent of all puppies have ridge but are heterozygous, and the remaining quarter lack ridges and are homozygous for lack of ridge.

(Note that it is theoretically possible,

especially in a small litter, that no ridgeless puppies are born; that statistical probability can lead us to think that at least one of the parents was homozygous for ridge.)

Option D:

		Parent A	
		rl	rl
Parent	R	Rrl	Rrl
B	R	Rrl	Rrl

This is what happened in the early days of the making of our breed. Dogs, whatever they really were, carrying a ridgelike hair formation on the back mated with regular dog types, i.e. without the hair formation. With one parent homozygous for ridge, the other (of another breed?) ridgeless, produced only heterozygote offspring, but all with Ridge. In the next generation, and assuming there was a reasonable number in the overall population, the early 'ridges' were here to stay. In that stage the ridged heterozygote dogs were likely to mate with some homozygous dogs with ridges, and you are at option B. Also, you had a number of heterozygotes mixing, adding the ridge population, as in option C. In modern society option D should only happen when a Ridgeback, through owner neglect, mates a dog of another breed. All

Option E:

		Parent A	
		rl	rl
Parent	R	Rrl	Rrl
B	rl	rlrl	rlrl

the offspring of this unwanted combination will carry Ridges on their backs.

This is another version of what happened in those early days (and a second alternative in a 'Ridgeback accident', this time with a Ridgeback which is heterozygous for ridge). From Option D we know that a dog which is homozygous for ridge-formation, mated to a normal dog, will produced offspring with heterozygous qualities for this formation, all still carrying ridges. Option E is what happened when one of these dogs, still carrying the hair growth on its back, met and mated a dog with no gene for a ridge-like hair growth. Half of the offspring still carry a ridge, but all of them are heterozygous for ridges, and the rest are ridgeless and homozygous for not carrying it.

WHAT TO DO WITH RIDGELESS PUPPIES?

There is a world of difference between culling purebred Ridgeback puppies without Ridges, and culling because of Dermoid Sinus. The old tradition among breeders has been to painlessly cull the ridgeless puppies immediately after birth.

Modern ethics are changing rapidly. An earlier chapter noted the mounting trends against dog ownership in society. The good news is that with any trend there is a counter-trend. Without going into specifics, e.g. the details of the Swedish pro-canine campaign, there is a positive trend, one for increased respect for Nature and all living things. In several countries this, among other things, means that younger vets refuse to put to sleep perfectly healthy puppies just because of a cosmetic problem. In some countries legislation has also changed,

securing better basic rights for dogs.

My position is that we should avoid producing so many Ridgebacks in any given society that we cannot find good future owners for all of them – including the ridgeless ones!

The people who would make excellent owners of pet dogs of Ridgeback origin, though lacking the Ridge, are normally different from those who might one day show, or even breed Ridgebacks. For instance, young people who are keen on dogs, who might be excellent Agility, Lure Coursing or Obedience handlers and who might not even be able to buy a top-quality purebred dog, can well have a ridgeless Ridgeback. The alternative would be that this young dog lover would, most likely, get a mixed breed dog.

I am also for the basic rights of mixed breeds, but I am not in favour of making a business out of breeding them. The reason for choosing a purebred dog, of any kind, is that you will know, with a rather greater degree of certainty than you would have with a mixed breed dog, what kind of a dog you are going to get. It is also a tribute to the companionship between man and dogs, which over thousands of years has evolved the various breeds, with their differing beneficial functions to perform in human society.

DERMOID SINUS

This is a potentially lethal syndrome that Ridgebacks (and sometimes other dogs) can be born with. It is, in a simplified explanation, a tube of hair, with an opening through the skin to the open air, growing into the dog, and in its worst cases reaching the dog's spine.

The possible hereditary percentages of this defect are not known. Experience (as reported by breeders in several countries) shows that some three to five per cent of puppies born carry Dermoid Sinus or DS, though this might vary from country to country. Recent Australian tests with Folic Acid, given to the bitch before the mating, have signalled a dramatic decrease in the birth of puppies with DS. It is also likely, following the Australian test methods, that bitches which either have a natural craving for foods (e.g. certain vegetables) that are rich in Folic Acid, or which will accept eating increased amounts of these products ahead of mating, should have decreased risk of producing DS in their litters.

DS can, in many countries, be operated on with significant chances of full recovery. Given the unclear hereditary causes, the fact that DS, if undetected in the very young puppy, will inevitably lead to suffering, and if not cared for, to painful death, is an acceptable reason for recommending that puppies with DS are put to sleep.

DS is most common on the back of the puppy, but is not necessarily confined to this area. The DS can be detected very soon after the birth of a litter, by systematically lifting the skin and feeling between the thumb and index finger for any tube-like elements growing in from the skin. DS can also be found on the tail root, on the skull and even on the flanks of a puppy.

Asking for assistance from an experienced breeder is a good solution for all new Ridgeback breeders who want to make sure their litters are properly checked for DS. Also the Rhodesian Ridgeback Club of Great Britain, has produced an excellent educational videotape about DS.

THE ROLE OF FOLIC ACID

A Preliminary Report on a Role for Folic Acid in the Prevention of Dermoid sinus in the Rhodesian Ridgeback, presented by John G. Roberts and Felicity A. Nicholls-Grzemski (Flinders Medical Centre and University of Adelaide, Adelaide, South Australia) at The Rhodesian Ridgeback World Congress, Melbourne, Australia, April 1996. Published with permission of the authors.

Dermoid Sinus ("sinus"), which can be single or multiple, was first reported in a Rhodesian Ridgeback (RR) in 1932. It has been the bane of RR breeders since that time and is widely believed to occur in approximately ten per cent of puppies. The true incidence has been obscured by the lack of a confidential reporting system and the reticence of many breeders to acknowledge its occurrence in their stock. Reputable breeders seek early diagnosis of puppies in the first weeks of life and euthanase or, on rare occasions, have the sinus surgically removed and the dog sterilised. Failure to remove a sinus leads later to cyst formation and potentially fatal infection.

Dermoid Sinus is categorised as a "neural tube (fusion) defect (NTD)" by embryologists. When the neural groove, which runs longitudinally along what will be the back of the developing embryo, deepens and joins to form the new spinal cord and spinal column, the skin of the back also fuses in the midline, and the spinal column and skin become completely separated. Partial failure of this process leads to Dermoid Sinus in the RR and to human defects ranging from "dermal sinus" (an identical condition) to spina bifida occulta (hidden) through to spina bifida cystica with serious paralysis. RRs do not exhibit this extreme form of NTD.

The neural tube fusion and separation process is complete in humans by day 35 post-conception, i.e. very early in the normal 280-day gestation period. As dogs have a 63-day gestation, this fusion (or failure of fusion) occurs within the first two or three weeks after conception. This very early establishment of any fusion defect is critical when considering possible preventative strategies. It is over and done with before pregnancy can be diagnosed reliably, certainly in the dog.

In July 1991 an immensely important research paper was published in *The Lancet* (UK). This was "Prevention of Neural Tube Defects: Results of the Medical Research Council Vitamin Study". This paper reported results which have changed world thinking on dietary folic acid (folate) – a non-toxic water-soluble vitamin-supplement before and during pregnancy. The study was based on earlier observations that lack of a nutritious balanced diet in the mother appeared to predispose babies to NTDs.

A large multi-country prospective trial was established. Women who had previously had a child with an NTD were recruited under strictly controlled conditions. These women were given one of four treatments which started before conception.

> 1. Vitamins A, D, B1-B6, C, nicotinamide
> or 2. Vitamins as above + folic acid 4 mg.
> or 3. Folic acid 4 mg.
> or 4. Iron/calcium

These were each taken daily until at least three months into the pregnancy. Maternal diet was not controlled. A definite result, i.e. whether the foetus/baby was definitely affected or not affected with an NTD, was obtained in 1195 pregnancies. The study was then stopped because the results were so totally clear that the study could not ethically continue.

The incidence of neural tube defects in pregnancies of mothers in either of the two folic acid groups was reduced by 72 per cent compared to the incidence in the non-folic acid groups. This information has revolutionised perinatal nutrition guidelines. The USA has recently mandated folic acid enrichment of basic grain-based foodstuffs.

This led one of us (JR) to wonder why this unique advance in human medicine might not be applied to a similar condition (sinus) in the RR.

The collaboration of a research pharmocologist/toxicologist (F.N-G.) was arranged. After approval by the RRCSA a prospective open study was promoted personally, in lectures and in dog club journals. A detailed questionnaire was forwarded to interested parties. It was left to respondents whether or not they supplemented their bitches' diets with folic acid 2.5 to 5 mg/day from the time of mating if not earlier. Details of average diet and history of sinus in the breeding pairs' birth litters were enquired of in detail. Respondents reported, inter alia, litter size, sex of puppies, occurrence of Dermoid sinus and any other congenital abnormalities.

RESULTS
To February 1996, reports of 51 litters comprising 429 puppies had been received.

Subsequent reports will be included in our definitive paper for publication.

Bitches on a "normal" diet (meat, bones, scraps, commercial dog food) produced 25 litters (213 puppies), bitches receiving a high folate (high vegetable) diet calculated to yield at least 200 mcg folate/day had 11 litters (93 puppies) while folic acid tablet supplemented bitches (15) had 123 puppies.

"Risk" of sinus, based on sire and dam's birth litter sinus incidence, was rated as "high" (sinus in the birth litters of both), "medium" if one parent's birth litter was affected, "low" if neither's birth litter had sinus, and "unknown". There was no correlation between perceived risk and the occurrence of sinus in the puppies reported in this study.

The incidence of sinus in the "normal" (low folate) diet group was 16 per cent. The two high folate groups (diet or tablets) combined showed an incidence of sinus of 4.2 per cent. In the high folate diet group zero incidence of sinus was reported. The folic acid supplementation by tablet group had a sinus incidence of 7.3 per cent (Table 1).

All the differences between the incidence of sinus in the low folate control group and that in the high folate groups are statistically significant (Wilcoxon rank-sum test, Mann Whitney U-test).

DISCUSSION

The results clearly indicate that high folate levels in the diet of the breeding Rhodesian Ridgeback bitch lead to a significant and important reduction in the incidence of Dermoid Sinus in the progeny. This is analogous to the proven situation in man. A reduction of around 70 per cent can be reasonably expected.

The small sample of high vegetable folate litters reported a zero incidence of sinus, while litters receiving folic acid tables showed a 55 per cent reduction. Why might this difference exist? The answer is unlikely to relate to other vitamins in the vegetable diet as this was not the human experience. It is most likely due to the fact that high folate diet bitches received a continuous and automatic supply of folate during their adolescence, sexual maturity, mating and pregnancy. No one had to remember to start tablet administration or to continue it on a daily basis – all the very limited body stores of folate would be continually full as would the developing ova. The converse applied to the folic acid tablet supplementation group where the time of starting treatment in relation to the bitch's cycle was sometimes not as recommended. Two bitches included in the folic acid tablet group were started on tablets at one week and ten days post mating (too late), while another bitch included in that group was commenced "on confirmation of pregnancy" (far too late). These inclusions in the folic acid treatment group can only have reduced the observed 55 per cent protective effect, which would have been expected to be higher in the face of timely or continuous supplementation.

CONCLUSION

High maternal folic acid intake in the preconceptual period and early pregnancy greatly reduces the incidence of Dermoid Sinus in Rhodesian Ridgebacks just as it reduces the risk of related conditions in man. A strong case can be made for either a high folate diet or continuous folic acid supplementation of "normal" diets throughout the reproductive life of RR bitches.

COMMENTS

The Australian study is, no doubt, interesting enough to warrant recommending Folic Acid inclusion in the bitch's diet prior to mating. What seems unanswered is whether *all* Ridgebacks have a predisposition to DS, with a lowered likelihood through the use of Folic Acid, or if these are individuals with an hereditary predisposition for DS, possibly influenced by Folic Acid. In this light, I support the view of the unanimous attendants at the 1996 World Congress in Melbourne. This position was taken in response to a question posed, via me, by the French RR breeder, Mr Bruno Hachet. It was that "Ridgebacks operated on for DS should not be awarded prizes in the show ring, neither should these individuals be used for breeding." One might add a serious caution against using individuals, born in DS litters, in breeding.

HIP DYSPLASIA

This exists in Ridgebacks, as in almost all dog breeds, but it can be kept under control with systematic X-ray and transparent information programmes. Draconian formulae with uncompromising rules and bans have not proved to lead to better overall results than more flexible information and education-based principles. Breeding, under controlled circumstances, with borderline cases, is correspondingly not proved to form a risk to the overall HD percentage. Countries with HD levels higher than approximately 5 per cent should pay special attention and might need stricter programmes, ideally linked to a specific objective, after which flexibility must be reintroduced. This also assumes that all individuals are X-rayed and the complete results publicised.

Already common sense says that buyers should be aware of the HD status of the parents, and ideally also the grandparents, of the puppies they are interested in. It might be close to naive to comment on ID rules, but better safe than sorry. Any HD X-raying system assumes that the national ID

TABLE 1

	No. of Pups	No. of Sinus	Incidence	Prevented Fraction	Significance
Folic acid tablets	213	34	16.0%		
Untreated (normal diet)	123	9	7.3%	55%	P = 0.03
High folate diet	93	0	0%	100%	P = 0.0003
High folate any source	216	9	4.2%	74%	P = 0.0005

routines are correct and that the ID is always marked on the radiography films.

The HD debate and action programmes, in a broad perspective, highlight two facts. First, that a systematic fault detection programme is needed and must be fully transparent; and, second, that neither over-focusing on single, hereditary problems can be detrimental, as the one-eyed focus can detract from other important issues. I suggest that HD programmes are essential but no excuses for, for instance, clubs grabbing unproportionate influence over individual breeders' right of self-determination.

OTHER DEFECTS

These can exist, and can also vary from continent to continent and country to country. The most important role any dog club can perform is to monitor developments in the health sector, systematically to gather facts when problems occur, and then to confer with genetic experts as well as sister breed clubs in other countries, both of which are likely to have experience and advice to offer.

The Grand Old Man of FCI and European research on genetics and hereditary diseases, Professor Sakari Paatsama, who passed away in the spring of 1998, detected ages ago, as an example, links between kinky tails and problems in the spine. Significantly, one of his final messages – he was active to the very end of his half-century long career – was that overprotection has not produced the expected results.

Another way of saying this is that hysteria over newly-detected real or imaginary problems does nothing for the breed. On the other hand, what we need and must demand from all clubs, not least all Ridgeback clubs, is absolute neutrality, an uncompromising willingness to act as information sources, plus a never-ending respect for individual owners' and breeders' willingness to listen, to learn and to act by themselves.

11 THE RIDGEBACK WORLDWIDE

The intention is to help readers understand how to assess dogs from various countries and to be able to check the pedigrees of some of the interesting dogs shown in the pictures in this book. This wander through the Ridgeback world starts in Europe, moves over to Australia and then to the US, comments on other regions where information exists, and ends, in Olympic tradition, with the Ridgeback's home country, Southern Africa. These dates, facts and suggestions came from a large number of sources. The provision of information has, in most, though not all, cases, been enthusiastic and generous. However, the source material has undoubtedly been somewhat variable in approach and style.

AUSTRIA

Austria has the honour of starting our country-by-country discussion. This country of 8 million in habitants offers magnificent natural countryside to the active dog lover. The first Ridgebacks were imported in the 1950s, though not officially registered. The first two names in the registration books are the African imports

Standing on straight forelegs gives any dog the perfect starting point for balance. Sarula Forosi also shows solid hind angulation, correct head proportions and a good expression.
Photo: M. Bernkopf.

It has been emphasised that good movement is where a quality Ridgeback begins or ends. Ch. Marunguela's Nanganura presents movement at its best, with long, low strides, active wrist movement, and an overall lightness in motion. Also note the correct position of the tail-root.
Photo: K. Vogelsinger.

Huntridge Amedeus and Glenaholm Lalela (Yaligimba's Budi ex Glenaholm Khanya) in 1977. Lalela is still seen in many an Austrian pedigree, and her son, Mtubatuba's Ambul (by Glenaholm Yuma), was the first Austrian-bred Champion, and was also a World Winner in Dortmund. By 1997 the club had registered its 300th Ridgeback and estimated that there were over 200 dogs in the country at that time.

This population is felt by the club to be rather heterogeneous, as indigenous breeding has not been active, in relation to imports. Over the years Ridgebacks have reached Austria mainly from Africa, Switzerland, Germany and Italy. The good side is that the genetic variety is broard and hereditary problems caused by close breeding have been successfully avoided. The club only accepts breeding from HD-free stock. The club correctly notes that, as only some 40 dogs have been X-rayed so far, statistical significance can be questioned. However, it is interesting that of the Austrian-bred Ridgebacks X-rayed, all but four have been HD-free, with four individuals showing a borderline case. Some imports have unfortunately shown clinically significant cases of HD. In 1996 the club launched mandatory X-raying of

elbows and shoulders, in order to prevent osteochondrosis.

Dogs to be used for breeding also have to pass a breeding suitability test (Zuchttauglichkeitspruefung), where they are checked for deviations from the Breed Standard and where a simple form of mental test is carried out.

Most Ridgebacks in Austria are kept as companion and family dogs, though there are examples of working and hunting with Ridgebacks, as well as some good results in Agility. The club arranges one club show a year, plus issues three membership bulletins annually.

The World Show in 1986 was held in Vienna, and in 1996 Austria shared the honour with Budapest, which hosted the Ridgeback part of the Championships. Austrian Ridgebacks have also competed internationally with significant success. In addition to the breakthrough wins of Mtubatuba's Ambul, other dogs of note are International and multichampions Gilah von der Ybbstalheide and Sakwi della Cime Bianche; Mehanna's Mataco, International and multichampion, plus top-winning Austrian Ridgeback; Mehanna's Macumba, World Winner and BOS in Budapest; Ctoret Beni's Ridges, international and

The most successful Belgian Ridgeback to date is Bundinas Cyrus, both International and French Champion. A strong head and a magnetic presence paved the way for his show results.

Photo courtesy: RRCB.

multichampion, and the top-winning Austrian Ridgeback, international and multichampion Mavunguela's Nanganura. The male International Champion Gabaza's Cabo has also competed successfully in France.

BELGIUM

Belgium, the small, trilingual country which has become the capital of Europe in political terms, is also the host country of the international Kennel Club, the FCI. The country, which has only existed since 1830, has about 10 million inhabitants and is known as one of the most dog-friendly countries in Europe, even if recent, entirely political moves have caused grave concerns for Ridgeback owners. There have been historic connections with the continent of Africa – Congo (Zaire) being the private property of the Belgian king until 1908. In Ridgeback terms, these are fortunate links.

The club is young, and was created by the enthusiastic family of Francis Materne and his wife Liliane Volont in 1992. The club's early history was founded on about 60 individuals, some of whom brought their dogs with them when they were repatriated after working in Zaire. By 1998 the club had some 150 members with about 300 Ridgebacks, which is a rapid growth. No doubt proximity to one of the power centres of European Ridgebacks, Holland, and also to France, has helped. The first club show was arranged in 1997, with the winners spread over three countries.

There are today no full-time professional Ridgeback breeders in Belgium. The club

This well-bodied bitch, Temba v. Masjonaland, is not only an International Champion, but is also active in Agility and Obedience. Note the depth of chest and the alert, penetrating glance.

Photo courtesy: RRCB.

has moved straight into a more Central European system of strict regulations for mating and club control of the litters. A major success story is the informal, educational Day of the Ridgebacks, held in magnificent natural surroundings such as the Soignes parks or the Ardennes. This event also includes an opportunity for dogs to pass a character test.

The first National Champion in Belgium was Mr Aenderkerk's Thembisa Khangeli, in 1991. In 1994, the Belgian-owned Temba v. Masjonaland, owned by Mr Materne, took BOB in one of Europe's toughest club shows, the Dutch RR Speciality.

CZECH REPUBLIC

The present structure of dog breeding and showing in the Czech Republic has only existed since 1993, a few years after Czechoslovakia gained freedom from the Soviet empire. Czechia has a population of 10 million people. This is a country which offers a lot of the very old – and a lot that is new. Kennel organisations had to be re-built. The average income of this ambitious nation, though rising rapidly, is low by European standards and an obstacle for quick expansion in the canine world. Czech civilisation goes back hundreds of years to Bohemia, which was a leading European cultural centre in the 14th century. This, in canine terms, means that the tradition of keeping different types of functional dogs is an ancient one. The proximity of Germany gives impetus to the new ambitions for building an active kennel organisation and a dog show culture. Both from a dog and a Ridgeback perspective, the recent work has been impressive.

Not entirely surprisingly the first Ridgebacks had already been imported before the liberalisation, in 1987. The Czechs never accepted that the Iron Curtain would stop them from being true Europeans. In that year Mrs Viktorinova, after enormous problems and using middlemen, as the communist regime did not allow travel to the West for dog

The Czech Ridgeback scene has developed fast, with several imports and an active show calendar. Mennystone's Shingi, a young male, has been picked to illustrate the fast-growing interest in Czechia. This dog shows muscular strength at a young age. Notice the solidly dark eyes, in keeping with the dark nose.
Photo: Mrs Brejchova.

purchases, obtained Merigal's Elanda (Nagaja's Eyk ex Merigal's Anouchka) from Mrs Pestalozzi in Switzerland. One of the unsung heroines behind this import was Lone Lorenzen from Denmark, and the first mating was between Torhusets's Tan Tally-Ho (Troldeborgs Dyero ex Troldeborgs Ehla) and Elanda.

The first RR club, KCRR, was founded in Brno, a city known for dog shows for decades. In 1990, in order to support the then Czechoslovakia, FCI gave the World Show to Brno. Today a second club, CKRR, also exists. The original club started a club show in 1991, with 11 dogs. In 1997 KCRR had an entry of 88 dogs. The new club, CKRR, also hosts club shows annually and one of their members' dogs, Ali Rodyrry (Dorian Ropotamo ex Bessy Z Africke Savany), was the top-winning Czech Ridgeback.

The Czech imports include dogs from Zimbabwe, Italy and Central Europe. The early success in attracting dogs from neighbouring countries to the shows means that the Czech clubs have taken off at an admirable pace. Whether the two-club set-up is a positive one remains to be seen. The CKRR has a different HD status approach to what we are used to, asking for a 0 for males, and maximum grade 1 for bitches. A character test is applied. DS is reported, though at a low level. Some breed club members are active in hunting and Agility with their Ridgebacks.

DENMARK

This ancient country, with just over five million inhabitants and an area some 30 per cent smaller than Belgium, has for years been the odd one out in the Nordic region. The rules and regulations of Danish society have always been more liberal than those in Sweden, Norway, and Finland. The land link to the Continent has also helped Denmark be more international than its neighbours. The fact that Denmark hosted the FCI World Show in 1988 and the European Winner Show in 1997 indicates how the kennel world has benefited from

The US-bred liver-nosed male Kwetu's Xoxa started a successful career, including a BOB at the tough Swedish Speciality, but tragically passed away at a young age. This picture shows a teenage Xoxa, already showing his strength of bone, a great expression and outstandingly strong feet. Photo: C. Tekirdali.

the close links to the rest of Europe. For years, dogs have been able to travel freely to and from Denmark, while Finland opened its borders only in the late eighties and Sweden and Norway in 1994.

The first Ridgebacks are known to have arrived in Denmark around 1965. Mrs Stenlycke produced six litters, starting at the end of the sixties, using her bitch Wawa of Owlsmoor. This number of litters from a single bitch sounds excessive in today's world, but we are talking about practice and customs 30 years ago. Mrs Stenlycke bred Boya (Zumbo Zimbawa ex Wawa of Owlsmoor) which became the first Danish Ridgeback Champion in 1974. The Danish RR Club held its founding meeting in 1982, brought about through the enthusiastic energy of Mr and Mrs Schrattenholtz. The first Chairman was Mrs Mette Kjaersgaard. The club has since lived through times of both peace and, if not war, at least turbulence.

The Danish club co-hosted the 1988 Ridgeback World Congress, which I chaired, and established it as a Pan-Nordic event, with hosts also from Finland and Norway.

In the show ring, the country has had a number of worthy names. The first known outside the country was the Schrattenholtz family's Kinghunter's Artus-Lionclaw (LouStigens Douglas ex Sanjika Nandiswaya of Janak), which also did remarkably well both in Obedience and in the Military Police training. The Danish and Nordic champion Tuasiwa's El-Chack H'Lobo (Makaranga Famous Chaka ex Torhusets Fairfax Ella) had six years of show successes, with four wins in the Danish RR of the Year contest.

The Danish-owned liver-nose Kwetu's Xoxa (Rusteau of Kwetu ex Kwetu's Belmont Lady) won the Swedish RR Speciality show, which, together with the Dutch show, is one of the toughest in Europe. The all-time top Dane has, however, been the bitch Kijasaman Dikimba Zuri (Mushana Jango ex Kijasaman Bine), bred by Mr Mogens Boerjesen and owned and shown by Soeren Holmgaard *(See Chapter Eight: What Made Them Great)*. This exceptionally elegant bitch has taken a World Winner title, with a BOS in 1994 plus two European Winner titles, four times Best Bitch in Denmark, and so on. She has also competed in Obedience classes I and II. Since those victorious years Danish exports have understandably been in demand.

Males should show masculinity and power in their heads, yet without coarseness and a heavy impression. The Danish H'Lobo offers us an example of a solid male head.

Photo courtesy: DRRC.

ENGLAND

This is the country that is the motherland of canine sports, with the Kennel Club being founded in 1873. It has also been the gateway for Ridgebacks entering Europe. There is little doubt that the first kennel organisation in the South African Cape area, already founded by 1891, was inspired by the English interest in purebred dogs. For the keen statisticians, we can also note that the first truly African breed to be shown at Crufts was the Basenji, in 1895.

The richness of the English kennel world has always been based upon the country's relatively large population, about 50 million in the English part of the UK alone, and its international thinking, which has survived the Empire. The downside, which starts showing up more and more, is the old-fashioned isolation, with rigid quarantine rules for imports. Even if some import regulations have been slightly eased, the real resurgence in English dog breeding will not happen until the country follows the Swedish-Norwegian example, proving that modern medicine and intelligent organisation can allow any country to open its borders for dogs. We outside the UK eagerly wait for this to happen – not least because the British dog world continues to produce innovations, such as the invention of Agility.

Jack Selby who, besides being an international judge, has done research on Ridgebacks in the UK, has discovered that the very first recorded Ridgebacks arrived in England in the late twenties. Mrs Foljambe, a big-game hunter, imported two Ridgebacks from Kenya in 1928. The first high-profile ownership came through the tobacco family of Mr and Mrs John Player – which is rather fitting, given the role that Ridgebacks have played as guard dogs for tobacco farms in Southern Africa. Mrs Player showed two Ridgebacks at Crufts in 1932. These were Lobengula (I'Nkosi of Avondale ex Vimy Ridge) and Juno (Viking Mondora ex Santalukela of Avondale).

After the horrors of the Second World War had passed, Dr and Mrs MacKenzie began to make an impression with their Mancross breeding. The first breed club, the Rhodesian Ridgeback Club of Great Britain, was founded in 1952 and two years later the breed got its certificate rights at Crufts.

In 1964 the Midlands and Northern Rhodesian Ridgeback Club was founded, and was later to become the first breed club

The UK Ch. Gunthwaite Corrina of Sonstraal is liver-nosed. Note the sculpturesque body and the extremely strong, well-muscled hindquarters.

Photo courtesy: S. Rossiter.

A strong male with a strong head, with that superbly alert expression that every judge should be looking for in the show ring. This is a breed born alert and should remain precisely that. Ch. Shabani Kana also shows solidly boned legs, with the correct oval (never rounded) shape.
Photo courtesy: G.&P. Regler.

that received Championship status in the UK. This development continued, and the Southern Rhodesian Ridgeback Association started its activities. Today there are also associations in the Republic of Ireland and in Scotland.

It has been recorded that Queen Elizabeth received a Ridgeback as a gift, and this dog, Just of Bamba (Rory O'Connor ex Larissa of Brabant), sired the first UK Champion,

Maiduba of Mancross (out of Larissa of Brabant).

The World Congress of Ridgebacks was held in England in 1992 and it continued the success stories of the 1984 and 1988 events. Many a continental Ridgeback owner felt that this was a door-opener both to, and especially for, UK breeders. The shows also grew rapidly in size, and 1994, when Sammy Wallace of Zimbabwe judged, there were a top 172 entries. Do note that the UK term 'entries' does not compare directly with the continental registration of entered dogs. In the UK dogs can enter more than one class.

While moving on to today's leading names, we must not bypass legends such as Mrs Woodrow's Mirengo's Mandambo with his record number of CCs *(see Chapter Eight: What made Them Great)*, and the Seaman family's Sansilver Senga (Kono of Owlsmoor ex Zaza Akeha), both of them showing wonderful length of body and securing this key feature for years, and Jack Selby's RSA import Ulundi Ushumba of Eilack.

The UK exports have been instrumental in creating quality lines in many countries. Among them are the Webster family's exports of Janak breeding, such as Penda

A male with a penetrating, curious expression. A long, elegant body and excellent angulation help make Ch. Nyassa Eiko a top-class Ridgeback.

Photo courtesy: S. Campbell.

Sana of Janak (Janak Piedt ex Suzereine of Janak), who made such a mark on Norwegian breeding, Janak Saara (Dannar of Janak ex Houghtonvale Kit of Janak), BOS at Crufts and mother of the all-time RR legend of Sweden, and Rooinek Jason of Janak (M'Kishi's Nallim Mhlekazi ex Janak Purdey of Rooinek), himself a Crufts winner, who also became the first Group winner in Sweden.

For the record-book fans, we should also mention one of the very few liver-nosed Ridgebacks so far to have won a Champion title, Gunthwaite Corrina of Sonstraal, owned by the late Bob Miller and shown by Sharron Rossiter. While we, in general, still do not know enough about the relationship between a liver-coloured nose and other features, the fact is that breeding a top-class liver is possibly the ultimate challenge in our breed.

The group of elite dogs in the UK includes: the RRCGB Championship Club show winner and the top-winning Ridgeback in the UK, Mr and Mrs Campbell and Wheeler's Nyassa Eiko (Gunthwaite Avenger ex Sheemar Sassi of Nyassa); the Club Open Show winner, Mr Harden's KweKwe Kumi (Burncote Baron ex Kweduve Kim); Mr and Mrs Agnew's Champion Mwenga Mgeni (Trendsetter Mtoko ex Mwenga Marijka); the Nyassa male Falco (Gunthwaite Avenger ex Sheemar Sassi of Nyassa); the Ringer family's Flametrees Ruby Tuesday (Sansilver Samuru ex Shona of Bunnockholm); and a very successful Irish and UK champion, Eddie Patterson's Tombezi Gypsy Girl (Rockridge Columbus ex Eber of Cloncrean). The UK has also seen a Dutch Vizara import climbing the ladders rapidly – Ch. Mangwe Llesha (Mangwe Kantua ex Mangwe Shamwa), owned by Mr and Mrs Baldwin, who won at Crufts, with the BOS going to Ch. Tukela Shona (Diamondridge Mkuki ex Tukela Zulu Dawn), owned by Mrs C. Joslyn. The majority of these UK winners show a modern, lighter-built type of Ridgeback, with good length of body and solid expression. The English scene is still one of international interest, while the country goes through a struggle to keep up with the rapid developments in the other countries which allow easy import of new bloodlines.

The UK clubs work along ethical codes for breeders. Since the latter part of the 1980s the HD scores are publicly available.

One of several significant UK exports was Nordustufial Liza of Janak, shown here with Betty Webster, one of the greats among UK Ridgebacks breeders. Liza was sold to the Maridadi kennels in Norway, where the Bringslid family made successful use of this bitch. Liza, like some of the other successful eighties exports, e.g Rooinek Jason of Janak and Janak Saara stood out from the majority of the British Ridgebacks of those days, with their excellent length of body. Getting the correct body proportions back into the breed has been notably successful in the UK over the past 15 years.

The RRCGB has produced both a Breed Standard video, and an excellent educational video on Dermoid sinus. In addition, the clubs actively arrange annual conferences, plus imaginative special events for fund-raising to the benefit of the rescue funds. The long list of UK judges that have judged Continental (and other) shows reflects the respect the country has earned through its years in the Ridgeback world. Many a European RR owner has shown for names such as Elisabeth and Wilf Webster, Jack Selby, Janet Parker; Trish Barber, Sue Simper, Julia Bates and Sue Wheeler, just to mention a few among many.

Finally a word about Standards. In the UK Standard, also included in the RRCGB Year Book of 1997, there is a printing error regarding the centimetre version of maximum height for males. The text claims 67cms, which should read 69. Unfortunately this printing error has had a rather grave impact in Central Europe, where it was not realised that this is a mistaken translation of 27 inches.

FINLAND

This small country, with about five million inhabitants, the largest uninhabited areas in Western Europe, and not merely thousands but tens of thousands of lakes, has been a slow starter in the Ridgeback family. The first Ridgeback was imported by Mr Lucander back in 1965, from old Swedish lines. That dog, Simba (in fact named Simba 5, after Simba 3 ex Suster 3, bred by the Swedish pioneer Bengt Floren), was followed by a female, Elona (Rhosaf M'Kimba ex Cora), born in 1975. She had a litter in 1978, but only two puppies remained in Finland. The first Finnish-owned International Champion was an import from the Swedish LouStigens Kennel, LouStigens Assam (LouStigens Haijk ex Janak Kelly), owned by Mrs Marita Laitinen. The Ridgeback judge, Leni Nousiainen, imported her first dog in 1974, LouStigens Bihscara (Roseridge Red Slim ex Janak Kelly), and later LouStigens Cama (Kungstorps Soleb ex Janak Kelly), both of which did remarkably well all the way up in the Winner Class in Obedience. Mrs Nousiainen lectured on Obedience at the 1988 World Congress in Denmark. 1988 was also the start-up year of the Ridgeback club, registering 15 members.

Later imports came from Sweden, England and the US. Mrs Marianne Aaltonen's UK import, Mbwa Jike Shinda Moyo, called Kimba, became the first Nordic Ridgeback to gain Championship status in Obedience. A great Finnish

Finland is the newest of the Nordic countries to breed and show Ridgebacks, but it is making rapid progress. Ch. Dahari Darubini is a bitch that could compete in any country. This is a Ridgeback of excellent balance, with solid angulation, correct proportions in head as well as body and strong feet.

Photo courtesy: RRCF.

Ridgeback success came through Mrs Aaltonen's import Shadyridge Mabruki Mbili (Shadyridge Fairviews Imba ex Shadyridge Nadra), exported by the Swedish-born US breeder Ulla-Britt Ekengren *(see Chapter Eight: What Made Them Great)*. Mbili won the BOB and World Winner title in Brussels in 1995. The Finnish club has enrolled a group of young enthusiasts, working together with the pioneers. The club hosts annual speciality events, Obedience and Agility courses, Lure coursing and Tracking competitions.

The club has drawn up guidelines for a programme against hereditary diseases. All stock to be used for breeding purposes has to be X-rayed for HD. In the past, between 1988 and 1997, some 37 per cent of the whole Ridgeback population was X-rayed, with only 5 per cent showing HD. In 1997 16 dogs were X-rayed, none of which showed HD. With this background, the club has wisely gone for an open system of information, with no strict rules binding breeders.

The World Show held in Helsinki, with an all-time record entry in Finland for the breed, was basically a Norwegian-Swedish affair, but Junior WW male was Mika and Sari Paakkanen's Ikimba Nembo, bred by Marianne Aaltonen. She also bred Ch. Dahari Darubini (Shadyridge Mabruki Mbili ex Imbali Khangayo), Finland's top Ridgeback in 1996, who took Best in Show-5 in Tallinn, Estonia. The Finns have had something else going for them as well. Ms Vappu Alatalo and her Ch. Lord Calvert are also competing in the Winner class in Agility. In addition to which, Paeivi Rantasalo's Kingizi Bayana (Shadyridge Wazari ex Ikimba Kingaza) is a qualified rescue dog. From a slow start the Finns are getting up to (real Ridgeback) speed.

FRANCE

France is one of Europe's leading hunting countries, as well as a top nation in various dog sports, and in addition France is the most dog-friendly society in Europe. Dogs are always welcome in hotels and restaurants, no matter how many stars the establishment has and, in many cases, the hotels compete by offering free dog dinners, dogfood and waterbowl packages to guests bringing their dogs along. This dog-friendliness seems to remain, even despite some recent and dubious anti-canine legislation. France is a large country, both in population, with close to 60 million inhabitants, and in surface area, making it the second largest country in Europe after Russia. The French Kennel Club was established in 1882 and it arranges one of the most elegant outdoor shows in Europe,

Fuiga MeisKe v. Huize Laurillard.
Photo courtesy: RRCF.

French Ridgebacks have, in general, shown good ridges and this (imported) Thembisa dog is no exception. Notice the excellent length of this ridge, which goes way past the mid-point of the thighs. Photo courtesy: RRCF.

The stern expression of a Ridgeback sometimes gives the (false) impression of a dog to steer clear of. The dark eyes, the sharpness of expression and the black muzzle are charming but deceptive. Mata Hari de Teufelsort has been chosen as French representative.

Photo: Gad.

the yearly Paris-Longchamps show.

In spite of these excellent conditions for dog ownership, Ridgebacks have been introduced at a slow pace. One reason has, in fact, been the vast distances between the various parts of the country, leading to somewhat isolated breeding in the early days. The first Ridgeback was imported from the UK in 1951, Kali of Emasne. The breed got a real start when the Servant family imported animals both from South Africa and from the USA. In 1988 initiatives came from Mrs Maria Robertson, Mr Servant and Mrs Rey and Wintermantel. The French KC approved the club the next year. In 1997 the breed for the first time passed the 50-dog registration level and puppies are now both exported and imported in significant numbers. The club has introduced a so-called TAN test, a four-step temperament test, as a condition for breeding as well as for Championships. HD results are also a pre-condition for breeding as well as championships. Achieving a French Championship is a major challenge, as four certificates (CACs) must be gained, and one of these must be from Longchamps and one from a Specialty show. So far these titles have predo-minantly been taken by international top dogs.

The club supports activities in many fields such as Agility and also arranges a yearly club show, starting with one in Nevers in 1991, which has developed into a highly international event while still keeping a friendly atmosphere. The show scene is still dominated by visitors. In Nevers, in 1991, the legendary multichampion Vishala Kinghunter Lance took his first victory on French soil. In 1993 he wrote Ridgeback history by winning President Mitterand's cup for Best in Show at the Nevers International all-breed show. The German male, Merten, owned by Mr Weinmann (see Germany), won both Longchamps and Nevers in 1977, with BOS in both shows going to Djungelkatten's Kinghunter Liaison (see Sweden). The club also hosts four or five Specialty shows a year within international all-breed shows.

GERMANY

The re-unified Germany, with over 80 million people, a large geographic area with ample free space, and one of Europe's dominant Kennel Clubs (VDH), could easily be a real Ridgeback powerhouse on the Continent. Added to that, German is spoken in some 10 countries in Europe (though as a minority language in several), so the possibilities are all there. German Ridgebacks are of high international quality, though neither show attendance nor depth of quality is at the level one would expect. The main reason for this is an unfortunate split into three different clubs, with no mutual recognition across club borders for breeding purposes. The largest German shows are hence still smaller than the club shows in Sweden or Holland. On the other hand, there is great activity with imports, and general interest towards the breed is growing strongly.

The first German Ridgeback club, the Rhodesian Ridgeback Club Deutschlands, was founded in 1996 and is approved by VDH and FCI. The written objective of the club is to preserve the breed in its original shape and form. The club has a special ZZP, the breeding aptitude test, which aims at ensuring that only socially well-adjusted dogs are used for breeding. The test also

takes into account basic physical qualities, and the rules state that neither males nor bitches are used for breeding before 24 months of age. By the end of the eighth year of any bitch she should have carried no more than five litters. The club has paid special attention to the concentration on certain stud dogs, and states that every stud dog, after four successful matings, should have a one-year pause. As a special service, to be used by individual breeders, the club offers a five-generation pedigree analysis in order to judge inbreeding coefficients and possible hereditary issues.

All dogs need to present known HD, as well as elbow and shoulder status before breeding. (As an example, a dog with a borderline HD status of B can only be mated to an A, while light HD status C disallows the dog from breeding.) During the period 1993-97 a total of 95 Ridgebacks were X-rayed, with these results:

HD-A (free)	77
HD-B (borderline)	13
HD-C (light HD)	5
HD-D (medium HD)	0
HD-E (grave HD)	0

The osteocondrosis test (OCD) in elbows, which was voluntary until 1997, shows the following statistics among 28 individuals:

OCD-Free	21
OCD-Light 1	7

The corresponding statistics for the OCD check of shoulders, for 26 individuals, gives:

OCD-Free	24
OCD-Light 1	2

The RRCD has close to 500 members, among which 35 are breeders. The club can use space for information in the German Kennel Club magazine *Unser Rassehund*, and in addition it communicates with its members through membership bulletins and at special membership events. In order to achieve geographic coverage the club is divided into regional sub-organisations. The club programme also includes services such as training in handling, puppy meetings, breeding information, and making the arrangements, with VDH, for international as well as club shows.

Among the RRCD stars are: Umwuma Jani, World, European and International Champion; Umwuma Duke and Ruacana Batu (Umwuma Duke ex Gonja Tom Etthewide), both Bundessieger-winners (the VDH Bundessieger show is a German version of Crufts); the Top-Ten winner Zuritamu Imara *(see Chapter Eight: What Made Them Great)*, also Bundessieger, VDH-Europasieger and International Champion; Zuritamu Ibura, 2nd in the Top-10 plus VDH-Europasieger, Bundessieger and multiple club show winner; and the third litter brother, Zuritamu Imani, double club show winner. These three are all offspring of the 1995 Top-Ten winner of RRCD, Vishala Kinghunter Lance (see Australia).

The two other German clubs, Lowenhund Deutschland Rhodesian Ridgeback (LDRR), and Deutsche Zuechtergemeinschaft Rhodesian Ridgeback (DZRR) are also approved by VDH and FCI. The parallel club developments are not necessarily because of frictions within the VDH, but rather as the result of a verdict by the Supreme Court in Germany allowing several competing clubs in dog (and other) sports, as part of the

The highly successful German show male Zuritamu Ibura is a dog that almost seems to defeat the saying 'Nice guys seldom win'. Ibura is not only a dog of extremely pleasant character; he even shows that in his expression (not necessarily always an advantage in the show ring, where it is all about being instantly noticed). This elegant neck is a rarity in a male dog.

Photo courtesy: Roberto.

Zuritamu Ghajana, a balanced and strong bitch with good bone, a correct head and typical long lean muscles. Photo: H. Spengler.

It is generally thought that bitches have been (and presumably still are) the better hunters in the Ridgeback families. The bitch is light, still with superb muscular power and a body which hosts a sizeable lung capacity. The German bitch Zuritamu Gwanda shows a balanced combination of femininity and strength. *Photo: H. Spengler.*

interpretation of the Freedom of Establishment act. These clubs are internationally active, arranging ambitious club shows as well as working with VDH at international shows, and having some excellent show Ridgebacks.

One of the classic males from LDRR has been Mrs Rosy Brook-Risse's Makaranga's Famous Chaka (Shane ex Lulu a.d. Skaaprevier), which has won extensively around Europe. He is an International as well as club Champion, but has possibly had the bad fortune to be active at the same time as some other world-class dogs, thus preventing a long merit list from being even longer.

Mr Hans-Juergen and Mrs Sigrid Weinmann's Dutch import male, Merten (Vumba ex Jockular Jodi), climbed to the position of being one of Germany's top Ridgebacks *(see Chapter Eight)*. He is an International and multi-champion, with several club show victories both from Germany and from abroad.

In closing, the top German Ridgeback in the international show ring has been Mr Marek's Dutch-bred male Rydgeway's African Hunter (Besal Fatok ex Rydgeway Copper Coin). *See Chapter Eight.* The team of Mr Marek and Hunter gradually climbed the results-list ladders, to take an enormously popular BOB and World Winner title in Budapest in 1996. Hunter was among the top three dogs of all categories in VDH's Group 6 list. Hunter is both International and multi-champion, and moreover, in partnership with his owner and handler, would be a clear candidate for a 'Gentlemen in the Ridgeback Ring' title, should there ever be one!

IRELAND

Ireland's population of five million inhabitants, in relation to the United Kingdom, makes it one of the smaller European states. This is also true for its position in the Ridgeback world, though the ambition is there, as are the first concrete signs of a breakthrough.

The launch of an Irish club, engineered by William O'Connor, came at an inaugural meeting in June 1985. Rules were drafted, and Mr and Mrs Jack Selby from the UK were invited over for an open symposium, coinciding with the IKC show on St Patrick's Day 1986. The first Championship show was arranged in September 1986. Since the formation of the Irish club the same year, the Irish Kennel Club has registered 622 Ridgebacks. The total number of registrations declined as a result of the Ridgeback being put on the 1991 Control of Dogs act. This means that a Ridgeback must be muzzled and kept on a lead when in public places. The work of the club, with membership contacts and creative ideas, has led to a healthy increase of club members, despite the legal problem. The club runs re-homing programmes and participates in the UK club's rescue schemes.

The first Champion owned by a club member was Pretty Little Blanche (Gatesjig Lampon ex Mary's Pride), bred and owned by Mrs Carmel Clery. First to become a Dual Champion, that is Irish and UK, was Eddie Patterson's Tombezi Gypsy Girl (Rockridge Columbus ex Eber of Cloncrean), who also took the first Best in Show at an all-breed show in Ireland. The first international breakthrough, measured by receiving a FCI CACIB, was Joan and

Ireland is a small nation with a big competitor, England, next door. This has not scared the Irish, and Tombezi Gypsy Girl was the first to break the ice, that is, take both Irish and UK Championships. This rather tall, yet elegant, Ridgeback has also won a Best in Show in Ireland. Excellent length of body has made this bitch competitive in Group finals.

Photo: J. Crawford-Manton.

Dennis Boyd's dog, Bwaga of Kilsinroe (Carsdale Eberhard ex Fevata Yoruba).

The club issues a newsletter twice a year, and has moved onto the Internet with information. The Code of Ethics encourages X-raying for HD of stud dogs and bitches, under the British Veterinary Scheme.

ITALY

This colourful country has a climate that should suit all types of canine sports. A population of almost 60 million people, a burning interest in sports, and centuries of traditions with hunting dog breeds should be a fertile ground for the expansion of a breed such as the Ridgeback. However, the

The sleeping beauty among the large canine markets in Europe is Italy, where Ridgebacks have taken a long time to gain a foothold. Despite this and thanks to the determined breeding work of a single kennel, the Best Bitch and World Winner title back in 1986 went to an Italian representative, Rhea. This daughter of the all-time great South African, Shangara's Checheni, shows wonderful depth of chest, solid bone and a fine croup. Photo courtesy: The Austrian RR Club.

start was very slow, or, to quote the iron lady of Italian Ridgebacks, Mrs Giovanna Bacchini-Carr, from the very first Ridgeback World Congress, "The history of the Rhodesian Ridgeback in Italy is necessarily short." As an example of this, during the first 15 years after the introduction of the breed in 1968, only 42 dogs were registered with ENCI, the Italian Kennel Club: 24 of these were from three Italian-born litters, and only 18 from imports. On the other hand, the early imports came from absolutely the best bloodlines, such as Mushana Starr Jameson and Shangara's Checheni (see Southern Africa).

Mrs Bacchini-Carr's bitch Rhea (Shangara's Checheni ex M'Panis Russet),

one of the two bitches imported by her to her delle Cime Bianche kennels in 1981, took a World Winner title at the World Show in Vienna in 1986. The earliest import was in 1965 when Mrs Ricci imported from Rhodesia Mwala of Mpani (Mpani Rip of Colemore ex Mpani's Flame Lily of Stallis). The first Italian Ridgeback to win Championship status was Rosette of Mpani (Glenaholm Strauss of Inkabusi ex Mpani's Ilala of Goromonzi), bred by the legendary Mylda Arsenis.

Italian judges have been judging Ridgebacks in many European countries, such as France and Sweden and at the European Winners Show in Denmark. A book by the prominent hunting dog expert Mr Di Giuliani features Ridgebacks and the

One of the top Ridgebacks of all times in Italy, Multi Ch. Kaya Delle Cime Bianche (Sa Delle Bianche/Mahara Delle Cime Bianche), shows a firm profile and a determined look.

RR Club of Italy was founded in 1997. Despite the small number of dogs, Italian-bred dogs have done exceptionally well when exported.

NETHERLANDS

This is one of Europe's smallest nations, with a high population density of 15 plus million people on a small piece of land, and yet it has been one of the leading Ridgeback countries in Europe.

Ridgebacks go way back to end of of World War II. The first Ridgeback was brought in by a female pilot in 1946. The first Dutch litter was born in 1949 from two imports made by Mrs Goedhart-Bakker. In 1954 the first national Champion, Indoena van de Tafelbaai, got her diploma. Moving to the early seventies, Mrs Tresoor-Homan became the first Dutch breeder with an extensive breeding programme. Some years later, another of the early pioneers, Mr Roy Meersman, started his Ridgeback kennel which was to produce a number of show winner towards the latter parts of the decade. In the breeding programmes of both Mrs Tresoor and Mr Mersmann, the British Footpath bloodlines played a major part. Moving into the eighties, Ridgeback numbers increased,

notably with Mrs Resang- Groenewegen's RSA import Avondson Topper and his offspring.

Early World Champion dogs include: the 1989 winner, Mrs Jones-Schleisser's bitch Rydgeway Copper Coin; the male World Winner of the same year, Mrs Coppens-Janssen's Jock (Glenaholm Gavula ex Anouk); and Mrs Bubbert's and Mr Meersman's 1990 World Winner male, Foldsworth Thembani.

One of the classics among European Ridgeback in the nineties was Vumba (Nkunda Nxumalo Vir Die Simba Safari ex Glenaholm Roan) (*See Chapter Eight: What Made Them Great*). Born 1988, he only started showing as a two-year-old. In 1992 he took BOB at the World Show in Valencia. He was also one of the first Group winners at an all-breed show in Holland – a country with fierce competition – and second in Group in the Dutch Dog of the Year show. He has sired 18 litters, producing a unique streak of winning Ridgebacks such as Hunter, Milton and Merten (see Germany).

The breed club was founded in 1979, and it now has some 3,000 members, with approximately 120 active breeders. The official club policy on HD is that only dogs

Three Dutch Ridgebacks that show the continuity of good breeding. Pictured (left to right): Rydgeway Touch of Class, Rydgeway African Dawn and the legendary father, Jock, quadruple Dutch Winner and also German Bundessieger.

In connection with the 1988 World Congress in Denmark, Best of Breed went to Rydgeway African Dawn, one of the stunningly sound examples of the Dutch standards in the eighties. A long, strong body, long correct muscles and exceptional angulation made this bitch a model for future generations.

with scores HD-A and HD-B should be bred from. Dutch statistics suggest a relatively low inheritance dependancy of HD – down to 25 per cent. On the other hand, among X-rayed dogs, some 20 per cent show slight or considerable HD, which has made the Dutch club pay special attention to the issue.

SWEDEN
Sweden has over 100 years of Kennel Club traditions. The country, with its 8-plus million population, has also been the undisputed world leader in the development of consistent hip dysplasia radiography and statistics. From a Ridgeback viewpoint, despite early imports both in the thirties and the fifties, the

The neck and the front are decisive factors in creating the elegant balance looked for in a Ridgeback. Int. Ch. Simbashana's Givenchy is one of the modern Swedish females that have produced strong yet elegant front and necklines – and some excellent offspring, as well.
Photo: Helen Engfelt.

Ridgeback chronicles start with Flight Captain Bengt Floren's Kenyan import in 1961, Judy of Endrick (Lanet Everbright ex Kim of Endrick), and Golden Glory (Tigiri Pellinore ex Suster) in 1962. The Swedish Rhodesian Ridgeback club, SRRS, was founded in 1974. It has since then operated under the auspices of the SSD, the Utility, Spitz and Toy Dog Club, which is a central resource for some 80 breeds not large enough to build their own facilities in all areas. When the SRRS reached a membership of nearly one thousand it decided to form its own breed club under the Swedish Kennel Club.

The very first bloodlines in Sweden were closely interconnected. The first Swedish-born litter dates back to 1963, bred by Mr Floren. This litter produced the first Swedish and International Champion, Mr Olle Rosenquist's Duke. Also there were more imports, in the early days predominantly from the UK. Exports to the neighbouring countries started in the seventies, developing into a healthy two-way exchange in the nineties. The Danish multiple Copenhagen winner Kinghunter's Artus-Lionclaw, the first Finnish Champion LouStigen's Azzam and some of the early Norwegian breeding stock, all originated in Sweden.

Aakemba's King Armani Gi Fumo won the Swedish Top-Ten competition in 1997, one of the toughest RR challenges in Europe, at the age of two. Photo: Helen Engfelt.

Djungelkatten's Kinghunter Liaison: This bitch started her show career by taking both the World European Junior titles She then went on to International Championship and the VDH-European Winner title.

The first Ridgebacks competing in the Group finals, and also boosting the show attendance, started their show-ring careers some 20 years ago. The male LouStigens Douglas, from two UK imports, Int. Ch. Robbin of Janak and the BOS bitch at Crufts, Janak Saara, took some 60 show victories and, making a comeback at a mature age, became the first Ridgeback with a Best in Show-placing, this at the age of eight. His last Top Winning Ridgeback in Sweden title came the year he turned ten. In between, the Crufts-winner Rooinek Jason of Janak, imported and successfully campaigned by Lennart Andersson, became the first Swedish Ridgeback to win the Group in an all-breed show in the early eighties. Interestingly, Jason, who also sired the first Norwegian superstar and the first Best in Show Ridgeback, Mwindaji Wa Simba's Flattering Alfo, was both preceded and followed by LouStigens Douglas on the Swedish and Nordic Ridgeback throne.

The first internationally campaigned Swedish-born Ridgeback was the bitch Kinghunter's Cassiopeia-Lionstar (Gunthwaite Arrogance ex Sanjika Nandiswaya of Janak), also three times the Top Winning Swedish Ridgeback. She took victories in the Norwegian RR Speciality, Best in Show placings both in Sweden and Finland, and towards the end of her career she both won the French RR Speciality in 1993, in a thrilling competition against the Dutch legend Vumba, and took a Group-victory and Best in Show-placing some years later in San Marino.

The top-winning ever Swedish and European Ridgeback, Vishala Kinghunter Lance, competing with a Swedish registration and Swedish owners (see

Australia), never lived permanently in Sweden during his seven-year show carrer in Europe. The genuinely Swedish star, Carina Pergren's male, Parih's Ghali Mizungo (Safaris Mwene Mutapa ex Kinghunter's Daria Lionlife), copied Kinghunter's Cassiopeja-Lionstar in taking three consecutive Top Winning RR titles in Sweden, and later on added a 4th. Mizungo has also achieved impressive results in neighbouring countries.

He is, for instance, the first Ridgeback to have won the final at the prestigious Nordic Winner shows (arranged in turn by the Nordic Kennel Clubs – *see Chapter Eight*). Before him, the Norwegian-bred male Mwindaji Wa Simba's Classic Clyde (Gunthwaite Arrogance ex Kinghunter's Arnia Lioneye), shown by Ingela Wredlund, took Group 2 at the Stockholm December show, one of the toughest shows in Europe. Following Clyde, Veronica Gomes-Hansson in 1997 made history by winning the group at the Stockholm December show with the Australian import Bearstar Diamond Willow (Bearstar Ko ex Bearstar Chilian Willow). Bearstar Diamond Willow also took BOB at the Norwegian RR Speciality. AnnMarie Hilding's import-intensive Djungelkatten breeding has been amply rewarded in Europe, with Djungelkatten's Kinghunter Liaison winning the World and European Junior Winner titles, plus the Top Winning French RR title in 1997. And, as a crowning of Swedish breeding successes in 1997, Suzanne Falk's female Kalaharis Bubezi (Savanne's Ruben ex Ridgehunters Atene Vinci) took the European Winner title in Copenhagen.

The club has arranged Club shows since the early eighties, now with Championship Certificates. In addition to shows, the club has long supported Obedience through a parallel Top Winning Obedience Ridgeback competition. In order to reach out to the members, the club has gradually been divided into regional units, hosting local events and arranging shows. The publication *Ridgeback-Nytt* is published four times a year.

The club runs its own breeding advisory service, as well as a puppy buyer information function. The club's ethical codes follow the Swedish Kennel Club guidelines, based upon education, information and direction. A break-through decision came in the early eighties, when the breed showed some 35 per cent HD among X-rayed dogs. Instead of going for obligatory schemes and bans, the club daringly embarked on a scheme based upon mandatory X-raying plus information on the results. The HD percentage level dropped from 35 per cent in 1975 to under 5 per cent in 1983. This level, with further minor decreases, has remained ever since. This is presumably the best case-history, proving that information is an equal, if not a better way to achieve results compared to restrictions. The club has also stimulated voluntary testing and research in the areas of breed-specific behaviour and temperament testing.

NORWAY

Norway was the last of the three Scandinavian countries to get going with Ridgebacks. Today, less than 20 years from the start of Ridgeback showing and breeding in Norway, this country has caught up and is an equal competitor – in the friendliest of senses – to Sweden and

Denmark. Norway, with a similar population to Finland, is a small nation, but is a huge country. High mountains and deep fjords divide the country and make physical communication from North to South a tough task. The saying is that Norway would be Europe's largest country – if you flattened it out. Some Norwegians live in this scenic region in the North.

The initial development of the breed in Norway was based upon English dogs. Many years before the start of the breed club, some missonaries brought home dogs from Africa, but there is no record of them. Neither did the first Janak imports in the early seventies ever get used in breeding. The title of being the pioneer therefore goes to Stephanie and Sigmund Bringslid, Kennel Maridadi, who brought home Penda Sana of Janak (Ch. Janak Piedt ex Suzeraine of Janak). Penda also became the first mother of a Norwegian litter, in 1982, and the first Norwegian-owned Norwegian Champion. The Bringslids later went on to import the 1980 Best-Winning UK dog, Nordustufial Liza of Janak (Ch. Mkishi Nallim Mhlekazi ex Ch. Rhoda of Janak). Both bitches played a significant part in establishing the Ridgeback breed in Norway.

Another founding mother was Tor Erik and Unni Pedersen's import Kinghunter's Arnia Lioneye (Int. Ch. LouStigens Douglas ex Int. Ch. Sanjika Nandiswaya of Janak) in 1980, who joined their kennel, Mwindaji Wa Simba. She became an International and Nordic Champion and was the mother of the first Nordic Best in Show winner, Mwindaji Wa Simba's Flattering Alfo, sired by the Crufts-winning male Ch. Rooinek Jason of Janak. The

Norway, this spectacular country in the North, is an ideal country for many types of sports. Despite the cold weather, Ridgebacks have found the space, and freedom it affords, a wonderful environment.
Photo courtesy: Susan Clayborough.

subsequent male import of the Pedersen family, Nord. Ch. Gunthwaithe Arrogance (Ch. Rejan Mandingo ex Gunthwaite Kasuli) was of great significance, both for Norway, and also in Sweden, where he sired what would be the all-time most succesful bitch. The classic Gunthwaite head is still sought after in this region.

The club was founded in 1983, and I had the pleasure of being part of the enthusiastic team which started it. The RR club has so far operated as part of the KSS, the club for Large Utility Dogs, but having

This young and balanced Ridgeback male presents a nice tuck-up of the chest, a balanced croup and lots of masculinity. Exgate Faruk Boss is one of many examples of the Norwegian breeding quality that has developed over the past 20 years.

Photo: K. Kristiansen.

acquired about 200 members, an independent club was established in 1998. The club has for many years arranged a club show during the Whitsun (May) weekend, an event which now counts its participants in the hundreds.

The club has been fortunate to have members who, from the very start, have been keen importers. In 1990 the Norwegian Kennel Club took over the

Mwindaji Wa Simba's Flattering Alfo: This classic Norwegian male was the first to break the ice in a major show, by taking a Best in Show.

sperm bank that has existed since 1972. Norway is one of the world's leading countries in the utilisation of frozen semen and many breeders have taken advantage of this. Both Australian, Dutch and US strains have therefore been used in Norway. For international comparisons, it is interesting to notice that the biggest Ridgeback litter using artificial insemination has produced 16 puppies.

Dogs have been imported from Sweden, which dominates as an exporter, the UK, Denmark and Australia. Selective and sensible breeding and ambitious education progress from the club have kept the breed at a reasonable level in relation to a healthy demand. On average 70 puppies are born each year, which is significantly lower than the total demand.

In Norway the majority of the population has access to nature just beyond their doorsteps, and as winter is longer than summer in many parts of the country, Ridgebacks have had a chance to enjoy fresh winter terrain. There is ample evidence that Ridgebacks have few climatic limitations. Many owners use their Ridgebacks to pull sledges or for leash-skiing (standing on skis, being pulled by a

Exgate's Fantastic Gipsys Fully (left), and Jespah Alekzandr of Janak took the honours at the 1996 Norwegian RR Speciality. They are two of the significant Norwegian show dogs of the era.

Photo: T. Benjaminsen.

dog in ready-made ski-runs). Some people have used their Ridgebacks in hunting, but little is reported of the lessons learnt. In the city of Trondheim, the Ridgeback Oppigardens Hilda Handfast, after training in Norway, is working as a guide dog. Everything considered, this Southern African dog breed has shown an impressive versatility and ability to adapt itself to conditions obtaining as far north as above the Arctic circle. Agility and Tracking have been tried, and recently an all-Ridgeback team competed in an Obedience contest.

In Norway, dogs must be X-rayed, after 18 months of age, in order to pass for breeding purposes. The HD level is almost insignificant. On a voluntary basis members are also advised to X-ray elbows.

With the relaxing of the quarantine rules, Norway hopes for Continental participation in their annual shows and Norwegian dogs have started competing outside northern Scandinavia. The Norwegian-bred bitch Kamba Anatulinda's Azizi, owned by John-Sigve Berg, was the first Norwegian Ridgeback to become International Champion since 1993 when her mother, Ridgefaret's Cleopatra, received the title. The pinnacle of Norwegian Ridgeback showing came at the World Show in Helsinki, with the Best of Breed and World Winner Title awarded to Oddveig and Anders Markeset's male Krismidt's Elgeyo Bantu (Bowbridge Ndoto Mukundi ex Exgate's Exantippe Ridgie), bred by Reidun Kristiansen.

SPAIN

Spain is a large European nation with over 40 million inhabitants. The Spanish kennel world has hosted a number of international events over the past decades but is not yet marketing itself on the Continent as actively as some of the other Southern European nations. However, Spanish entries are becoming common in some big events. In 1992 the World Show was held in Valencia. In the 1994 World Show in Bern there were some Spanish Ridgebacks, as there are in some of the larger German Club shows. Some German and Swedish imports currently live in Spain. It should, on the other hand, be noted that His Majesty the King of Spain is a Ridgeback owner.

PORTUGAL

This, the smaller of the two countries on the Iberian peninsula, with a population of 10 million, got a quicker start with Ridgebacks. Portugal has recently done some excellent work in the kennel world. The European Winner show in Estoril,

outside Lisbon, in 1993 helped the good word spread around the Continent.

There is not yet a Ridgeback club in Portugal. Mr Cesar M. de Castro Martins imported his first Ridgeback from Mozambique in 1966. In the early eighties the total number of Ridgebacks was estimated at about 20. By 1998 the estimates had grown to above 200. In addition to the Portuguese breeding, there are also imports, including Glenaholm stock from South Africa.

A top-winning Portuguese Ridgeback was

Tyrone de Quinta de Ferdias, owned by Cesar Martins, who is related to a family which has spent many years in Africa, and who has himself lived in East Africa. He says "I love big game hunting, and I prefer dogs that are better for this purpose, that is, dogs not so tall, but very strong, powerful and agile." His present males vary between 66 and 68 cms, with a weight of 40 to 45 kilograms.

Finally, let us present the most international dog from Portugal, The Guardsman Bruce Lee (Glenaholm Moshesh ex Tezela de Chingola), owned by Pedro Costa Macedo. Bruce won Brazilian, Spanish, Gibraltar, Portuguese and eventually International Champion titles, taking 51 career Best of Breeds.

SCOTLAND

Scotland is a small, though tough, nation with about 5 million inhabitants, so the Scottish canine scene is dependent on its interaction with the British kennel world. The Scottish Ridgeback club is rather small, with some 160 members. The club is fortunate to have the renowned judge Dr Arthur Sneeden as Chairman, and the club is active, with two Open shows a year, Ridgeback walks, and a club newsletter to keep both show people and non-showing members active.

A top-winning Scottish Ridgeback was Jonathan and Anna Ringer's Champion Mursil Huntsmaster of Barca (Ch. Rejan Qualitaire ex Shona of Burnockholm). This winning male was followed by his team mate, Ch. Flametrees Ruby Tuesday (Ch. Sansilver Samuru ex Shona of Burnockholm), together with the Nelson-owned bitch Zougani Zapella (Ch. Jespah of Janak ex Zougani Aristata).

SLOVAKIA

The Slovak Republic is the smaller of the two parts that some years back formed Czechoslovakia. There are about 5.5 million inhabitants in this country that is so close to Austria and Vienna. The Slovak Ridgeback club was already in existence in 1994, which shows the interest and dedication of this

Ch. Ador Bukama was the most successful Slovak Ridgeback in 1997, winning both the Hungarian and Slovak Specialities. This is a masculine dog with good bone, and a strong yet not too heavy head. The white patch on the chest, some 15 years ago a cause of debate, is fully permissible, almost adding character to the dog. Photo courtesy: SKCHR.

The Dutch import Rhody (left) started the Slovak breeding; (right) Asanta Pacifik is also successful in 'New Europe', with International, Polish and Slovak Championships.

Photo: J. Micuch.

young nation. Today there are 55 members in the club, with an estimated total Ridgeback population of 65 dogs. The breeding started with a Dutch import, Mr Micuch's Rhody (Maharajah of Bo Kama ex Boikokobetso), and the Victorinovci family's Simba of Bo Kama. The present bloodlines stem mainly from European breeding, for example from Rydgeway Africana, Besal Fatoka and Mennystones Shingy. The first International Champion was Assio Zahoranka, who was also twice a Club show winner.

The Slovak club show is run in conjunction with the Czech club for maximum participation, and the judges are of international reputation.

POLAND
Poland, the largest of the new free-economy countries in Central Europe, with close to 40 million inhabitants, has both the space and the nearness to Germany to become a noteworthy Ridgeback country in a few years. According to verbal information, there are at least seven breeders in Poland, though the Polish Kennel Club had not yet reported the existence of a formal club.

SWITZERLAND
Switzerland, a small Alpine nation with 7 million citizens, is Europe's richest nation. While solidly nationalistic, it is in the heartland of Central Europe and in close contact with its neighbouring countries. The Swiss Ridgeback club started in 1980. Show activity is somewhat hampered by the fact that there are very few official dog shows within Switzerland. On the other hand, distances to the shows in the neighbouring countries are short and Swiss

Switzerland's first great star was shown to two World Winner titles, by the President of the International Kennel Club, FCI, Mr Hans Muller. Campolongo's Aranja was a lean, balanced, highly feminine bitch, with elegant, long muscles and a great length of body.
Photo courtesy: Hans Muller.

The internationally successful Merigal's Chipili, who was also a valuable stud dog. A medium-sized, balanced dog, with good ribcage, strong bone, good chest and correct angulation.
Photo courtesy: H. Henriz.

Ch. Kianga's Chivaz.

Ridgebacks have been frequent guests at the colourful Flower Coast Week of San Remo, Nice and Monte Carlo, and in other points North, West or East.

The first Ridgeback entered in the Swiss records was the male Valavran Chuck, imported from the UK in 1956, and the bitch Sandy, born in South Africa. These two dogs gave the pioneer Mrs Favre the honour of producing the first Swiss-bred litter, in 1957. Following one more litter, there is a gap in registrations until 1967 when two more UK Ridgebacks found their way to Switzerland. The first RR member-ship meeting took place the year the club was founded, in 1980 in Winterthur. No fewer than 47 members turned up.

The international breakthrough for Swiss Ridgebacks came before the club was formed. Mr Hans Muller's bitch, Campolongo's Aranja, won the World Winner titles in 1979 and 1980. Aranja produced the best known Swiss Ridgeback, the great Champion Kianga's Chivaz (Mtubatuba's Ambul ex Campolongo's Aranja). Owned and shown by Yvonne Schoenholtzer, Chivaz won another two World Winner titles for Switzerland.

The Swiss club has, in contrast to for instance Australia, Sweden and Finland, symbolised strong centralisation, and breeding has been controlled almost with an iron fist. Presumably due to the small number of dogs used in breeding, partly as a result of these rules, the development of the breed has not taken place at the expected pace. The general activity level of the club is high. Membership bulletins, breed reports in the Swiss Kennel Club magazines and special family events keep the members involved. The annual summer Ridgeback walk in spectacular scenery offers everything from barbecues to opportunities for testing dogs in track racing.

OTHER EUROPEAN COUNTRIES

Andorra, a mini-country that arranges dog shows, does not have Ridgebacks in its registers. The Kennel Clubs in Estonia and Lithuania report that no ongoing breeding exists at this point. Gibraltar has crowned a few Champion Ridgebacks, but they live in Portugal. In Hungary there have been some imports, though no organised breeding has started yet. Hungarian judges have shown great interest in the breed, and Dr Zuzanna Balogh has even judged in Australia. The Icelandic KC, which has been re-built after some terrible anti-dog laws a few decades back, notes that Ridgebacks do not exist and that their climate is hardly ideal for an African dog breed. The Luxembourg KC has no registered Ridgebacks in their

Israeli Ch. Dafni the 2nd is a solid example of the young Israeli Ridgeback breeding. Note the long, sound and strong shoulder muscles. Photo courtesy: Y. Pardo.

Austrian and Hungarian Ch. Ctoret Beni's Ridge is a succesful Israeli export. The classic, equal proportions between length of muzzle and skull are near to perfect. Photo: U. Lichtenauer.

records, neither has Malta, Monaco or Romania. Russia does have Ridgebacks, but the KC has no registered breeders. Information received at Crufts in 1998 suggests that Russian show circles are keeping an eye on our breed, and Russian Ridgebacks participated in the 1998 World Show. The Ukrainian KC said that it has had two Ridgebacks, which have now moved with their owners to Lithuania. No information has been received from Slovenia, Yugoslavia, Cyprus, Croatia, Bulgaria or Turkey.

ISRAEL
The ancient land of Israel, the home of about 5 million people, is in the unique position of being a Western style democracy in the Middle East. As is the case with several sports, for convenience we can include Israel under 'extended Europe'.

Israeli judges have made a good name outside Israel, and the Ridgeback enthusiast Orit Nevo is an authorised Ridgeback judge, who has judged, for instance, in the UK. Israeli Ridgebacks have, during the latter part of the nineties, been seen at many European shows, with considerable success. Israeli-bred Ridgebacks exist today, for instance, in Holland and France.

The first Ridgebacks arrived in Israel in the early 1970s. However, the first two Ridgebacks entered in the Stud Book were Shirory's Umzikulu and Shirory's Ndambi, imported from South Africa. The ongoing breeding in the country got its start when Brigitte and Uri Liberman returned to Israeli soil after many years in Africa. Mr Liberman's male Ridgeback companion, Simba, had even accompanied his master in elephant hunts. Besides the African lines, other older lines go back to Holland, some

Ridgebacks are gradually entering Central and Eastern Europe, at the same time as the canine sports are coming back after many decades of darkness in these markets. Many of the Ridgebacks are either imports or have been brought along by visiting businessmen. This male, Paul, symbolises the many known, as well as unknown Ridgebacks that will help build the breed in 'New Europe'. He has visited many countries, from Ukraine in the east to Lithuania in the west.

imported by the Degani family. Two kennels came out of stock bred by them – Ridgebar and Eli Rosh Pina.

The show breakthrough came on home ground in 1987, when Simba Ridgebar, bred by Haim Bar at the Golan heights, took the World Winner title and also won the Group. Another Israeli dog took the Best of Opposite Sex and World Winner title in Tel Aviv in 1987, Wisky Eli Rosh Pina, bred by Eli Sloves. The enthusiastic breeder and experienced handler Beni Kiesler has travelled the international show world. He started his breeding back in 1987 and had his breakthrough with the male Johokwe Golo Zeus (Makaranga Famous Chaka ex Juba Delle Cime Bianche). Zeus had a long list of successes. In his first ten years as a breeder, Beni Kiesler had 23 litters. Others breeders in

Israel include Michal Masad, and Mrs Orit Nevo who breeds under the Rich-Rach name.

The club started in 1980 and joined the Israeli Club for Bigger Breeds. The initiative of a RR Winter Show started in 1988, as an unofficial show judged by me, and already by 1990 the Israeli enthusiasts had encouraged Sammy Wallace from the Parent Club to judge. The Israelis have done well and many tales that stun the Western world have occurred. Despite the extreme climate and the hostile neighbours, canine life goes on and goes upwards. As an example of the challenges that confront our breed, the breeder Gilaad Liveni from the Aarava desert reported that one of his males was bitten by a cobra-type snake – and survived.

THE FAR EAST

The Far Eastern nations report that there is, as yet, little activity as far as Rhodesian Ridgebacks are concerned. For instance, Japan notes that Ridgebacks have not yet really caught on, despite some imports. They also added that the kennel world of Japan might not be ideal for the breed, which is true when you think about the enormous shortage of free land there. Korea has not registered organised breeding of Ridgebacks. There is information about some imports (e.g. from the UK) of individual Ridgebacks to Sri Lanka. The Singapore and Hong Kong organisations had no registered Ridgebacks, though dogs have been imported to these nations. We do not have information about Malaysia (Ridgebacks have been exported from Australia to Malaysia), Indonesia, India and Thailand. The latter has a number of

A lean, yet muscular male, shown in top muscular condition. Ch. Vishala Sikoto won Best of Breed among almost 250 Ridgebacks at the Speciality in connection with the 1996 World Congress in Melbourne.

A good and long neck is not only essential for elegance in bitches; this male, Ch. Skiska Solitaire Jest, has a masculine head with a long, powerful neck and solid bone.
Photo: S. Stasytis.

breeders of the so-called Thai Ridgeback, some on a fairly large scale. It should, however, be repeated that this dog has nothing in common with the Rhodesian Ridgeback, except for a rather undefined hair formation on the back, and this book will draw no parallels whatsoever between the two different breeds.

AUSTRALIA

This is the only country in the world that is a single continent and, with a surface covering some 7.2 million square kilometres, the distances are enormous. All in all under 20 million people live in this vast land. Enthusiasts from Western Australia, as an example, needed two to three days to reach the 1996 World Congress and Jubilee show in Melbourne. Those who came from 'around the corner', in Aussie parlance, had an eight-hour drive back home to Sydney. The consequence of this is that independent and well-functioning clubs have developed around the country. The quarantine laws are also among the toughest in the world and as a result few breeders have a chance to use imported bloodlines to the extent that is possible, for instance, in the US or on the Continent in Europe. Exports exceed imports, and the impressive reality is that Australian Ridgebacks have turned out to be exceptionally successful abroad, both in the show ring and in breeding. We will also find that the RR circles in Australia, like those in Canada and the US, are more versatile and test Ridgebacks in far more places than just the sofa or the show ring.

Almost a full century ago a group of nurses who had returned from the Boer War were shown in a picture with a dog named

Buller. The Boer War was fought almost two decades before the official foundation of the Ridgeback breed, but the dog in the picture resembles present-day Ridgebacks enough to be picked out and recognised as an early precursor of our breed. It is also difficult to refute the statement that Buller was the first of his kind to set paws on Australian soil.

In the 1930s, a Mr Kostner, presumed to have been a life member of the Parent Club in Rhodesia (today's Zimbabwe), is said to have stopped over in Queensland during a round-the-world sailing tour. There he swapped a Ridgeback for an Australian Cattle dog. Many a Ridgeback lover would have seen this as a good reason to cancel the life membership! No documentation has been found, but Mr Kostner's widow has confirmed that, in fact, two Ridgebacks were left in Queensland and that her late husband had stayed in touch with their new owners for many years.

Around 1964 a couple bought a Ridgeback bitch from Dr and Mrs McKenzie of the Mancross kennels in England. They took the dog with them either to Queensland or New South Wales. They did not apply for a pedigree, thinking their pet was the only Ridgeback in Australia. Later on they heard about a male in Western Australia – believed to have been M'Bile – but he was too far away to be considered as a partner. And that is the end of the description of the early years, as provided by the three ladies Sadler, Hanks and Carson.

In 1966 Mr and Mrs W.M. Adams emigrated from East Africa to Western Australia, taking with them the above-mentioned M'Bile, imported from Tanzania. This was the first officially registered Ridgeback. Unfortunately the dog died soon after leaving quarantine and no breeding had been started. In 1967 Mr and Mrs Adams imported the dog and bitch that should have formed the start of the Serengeti lines in Australia. They were Serengeti Meru and Serengeti Chala, bred in the UK. They were half-brother and sister and became the first Ridgebacks to be shown. This piece of history was written in Perth at the Royal Show of 1967. Only one male survived from this pair. Mrs Connie Churchill, who also had two UK Ridgebacks and who operated the Sikota kennels for some years, owned him.

The first Ridgeback to travel to the

Ch. and LCC Makimba Taima Indodakazi, both a top Lure Coursing RR and a Best Headed RR in the Speciality. Note the strength of muzzle, the dark eyes and the correct ear setting. Photo courtesy: RRCQ.

A natural environment for a healthy Ridgeback – Aust. Ch. Malachi Mitonda on stock and guard duty. Note the high tail root, signalling maximum attention, as well as the almost bird-dog-like signal with his right front paw.
Photo courtesy: RRCQ.

Australian East coast was Serengeti Sanya from the second Serengeti-litter, born in 1968. Mr and Mrs Morris of Kellywille owned this bitch and she became an Australian Champion. The first Ridgeback to go to Victoria was also from the second Serengeti litter. Serengeti Mara was owned by Ms Janet Murray (the well-known Ridgeback author, earlier active in South Africa, who has been breeding under the Ulundi prefix), and Serengeti Sambu by Mrs Nina Bieberitz (breeding under the Bulawayo prefix). Sambu later became the second Australian Champion. Janet Murray went on to possess Owlsmoor and Aldonnels dogs from the UK, and Debassa of Owlsmoor also became the first imported Ridgeback to win the Champion title.

Between 1969 and 1972 there was a total ban on the importation of livestock to Australia from anywhere but New Zealand.

During this period the Australian Ridgeback population grew to some 300, all originating from six imported individuals. After 1972, there has been noteworthy import activity, considering the hardship importers and dogs must undergo. Among the special Ridgebacks which have earned Championship titles in more than one country are US and Australian Champion Calico Ridged Commander Cody, owned by Mr R. Leys, and South African and Australian Champion Komkhulu Nkazimlo, owned by Mrs Temmlett. These great dogs are no longer living, but both have contributed greatly to the Australian Ridgeback scene.

There have also been major advances in the use of artificial insemination. In recent years, semen from the US has been successfully used in several states in Australia. Today Australia together with Norway, is one of the world's most experienced and successful users of artificial insemination.

As mentioned above, exports have been significant, and include countries such as New Zealand, Hawaii, US, Canada, RSA, Zimbabwe, Malaysia, Singapore, New Guinea, Japan, Hong Kong, and Europe, notably Sweden. Australia has also produced two Ridgebacks which have become International Champions, one exported from the West, one from the East.

The Australian breeders note that the show ring fortunes of Ridgebacks in Australia have varied. The problem, not unknown to many younger Ridgeback countries – in which we do not count Australia – is that often judges are not familiar with the breed, and, as a result, quality Ridgebacks in sometimes mediocre

This Ridgeback bitch clearly follows the stance of the famous symbol on the South African Kennel Club emblem: Standing high with the front, watching the surroundings with an intense gaze. Ch. Vishala Inkosi was a female with exceptional power, yet absolute elegance. The front is also a textbook example of how a Ridgeback should be constructed.

Group line-ups have been invisible. Today a larger and larger number of Ridgebacks is being shown and, over time, more and more breed representatives have been receiving Group or Best in Show awards.

The Ridgeback has finally really arrived on the Australian show scene and it is there to stay. Serengeti Meru won the first Group award back in 1968. The first in-Show merit went to the brown-nosed bitch Sikoto True in the same year, both in Western Australia. The first Best of Group Winner was Mandingo Mandouma in Darwin in 1974 and later the same year this male went runner-up Best in Show. It was in 1980 that the coveted award of Best in Show fell to a Ridgeback. This breakthrough came in Victoria, where the Etosha kennel's UK import, Asayala M'Toto of Chima, took the top award.

Specialist Rhodesian Ridgeback clubs have been formed in New South Wales (1973), Western Australia (1981), Victoria (1985), South Australia (1988) and the Australian Capital Territory (ACT). That last one was re-constituted in 1993 after having been a sub-group of the Hound Club. There is also an unaffiliated club in Victoria (1992). All clubs have a high activity level, including offering point scoring competitions, racing, Lure coursing, Obedience, Agility and social programmes. The Hound Club of the ACT has regularly contracted expert judges for the Ridgeback section of its April Championship shows, and the NSW and Victoria clubs have arranged Championship shows for a number of years. The Western Australian club conducted its first Championship show in 1992 and the South Australia and Queensland shows started in 1994. The formation of the National Rhodesian Ridgeback Council, covering Victoria, Queensland, South Australia, Western Australia and the ACT clubs, in 1989, paved the way for the National RR Specialty Shows. The first of these, hosted by the NSW club, took place in 1992. It attracted over 200 dogs and the historic first winner was Aus. Ch. Marsabit Mfumo, bred by Pauline Sadler and Pat Clancy-Worrell. (*See Chapter Eight*)

No picture of Australian breeding achievements would be complete without describing the most successful export, whom we have mentioned earlier, Vishala Kinghunter Lance (Sansilver Mandambo ex Ch. Vishala Inkosi) bred by Deidre Bacon and Katie Hawkins in New South Wales. This male, born in 1990, took the European Junior Winner title in 1991 and his first CACIB at almost exactly 15 months, the minimum age. His breakthrough came at the 1991 French club show, where he took Best of Breed. Then followed a Vice-World Winner title in 1992, the European Winner title in 1993, World and European Winner titles in 1994, the vice-World Winner and, a third European Winner title in 1995, plus his International Championship and also no fewer than 12 national Championships. He was the first Ridgeback to win Best in Show at a French international all-breed show and he has numerous Group wins in several countries, a long list of Group placings, and CACIBs in 15 countries. He continued winning when he passed the age of eight and entered the Veteran classes. He took all of his wins flying the blue and yellow Swedish colours, though most of his wins came when residing in Switzerland.

OBEDIENCE TITLES

Ridgebacks in Australia in Obedience are no strangers to success. The basic Obedience title of CD (Companion Dog) is frequently awarded to Ridgebacks. A number of Ridgebacks have progressed to CDX (Companion Dog Excellence) level and even a few that have reached UD (Utility Dog) status. Ch. Glenrowan Alana, trained and owned by Mr and Mrs M. Price, became the first CD Ridgeback in 1974. Ch. Laughing Willows Kalarooi took the first CDX and the male, Zion, owned by Mr John Connell, was the first to reach the UD heights. Mr Connell's Jedda has also taken a UD, and Malcema Korina, owned by Brian and Rosie Coppin of South Australia, has achieved the third such distinction. Korina is also a TD, the first Ridgeback with a Tracking title. Baeimooi Caller Mel, bred by Nanette Rothman of Queensland, owned and trained by Kath and Les Spicer, is an Australian Obedience Champion (AOC). A number of Australian Ridgebacks have passed the Endurance test, the first of them being Ch. Trezridge Tembu, owned by Rob and Di Jolly in South Australia. The first to reach the AD (Agility Dog) title was Ch. Chamwari Impi, owned by Austin and Sandra Taylor of Western Australia.

AUSTRALIAN BREEDING ETHICS

Ridgebacks are the fastest growing breed in the Hound Group, even when counting the six Dachshund varieties together, which, naturally, poses new challenges for the Australian Ridgeback organisations. The question of balancing interest and demand

Pictured (left to right): Heronhill's Yuranga and Heronhill's Wind Wakker, both Champions, have proven the stamina of Ridgebacks by participating in the Canadian Iron Dog Triathlon, both coping excellently. The dog to the right deserves his full title. He is UCD, UCH, DC Ddnali's Jomo Wa Krinyaga, CD, MC, LCMZ, SGRC, SRM, TT, CDC and VC – a world record title?

Photo courtesy: RRC.

with buyer selection and supply is an enormously touchy one, as has been mentioned earlier with regard to Norway.

As an example of breeding ethics, the breeding programme of the RR Club of Western Australia assumes that a breeder who is a member of the club should breed only from registered Ridgebacks which conform to the Breed Standard, have been X-rayed for HD and are believed to be free of major hereditary defects, and mentally and physically sound and not suffering from acute nervousness or aggressive tendencies.

It is expected that bitches will not be used for breeding prior to two years of age and will not be bred from on consecutive seasons or over the age of seven years. No bitch should be expected to produce more than four litters or forty pups in her lifetime. Should a breeder feel it necessary to go outside these limits, it is anticipated that the opinion of a veterinarian is sought first. All puppies are carefully examined for Dermoid Sinus a few days after birth and at least twice thereafter before leaving for new homes. Any puppy discovered to have DS before leaving the nest should be humanely put down. (It must be noted that not all vets in all countries are in agreement, but that they rather recommend an operation (*see Chapter Ten*).

I have highlighted these principles as they are very close to the ideal balance between stating responsibility, respecting personal and membership integrity, and offering

Ch. Rindurr's Kmili Kweli Rafiki, proudly exposing his magnificent front, elegant neck and strong feet. A perfectly balanced Ridgeback.
Photo courtesy: RRC.

common sense solutions to ethical issues facing breeders.

CANADA

This vast country, with huge tracts of untouched terrain, is in a sense a dog lover's dream. The population of Canada is barely 30 million. The area is 9.2 million square kilometres, making Canada the second largest country in the world after the Russian Federation, which has 17 million sq. kms but 150 million people.

The popularity of the Rhodesian Ridgeback in Canada, which was high directly after the Second World War, has risen and fallen in different parts of this enormous country. The first Ridgeback club was started up in the early 1970s in the West and covered all of Canada. Due to difficulties in holding meetings and getting close to the membership, the club was unable to thrive. Late in the same decade three clubs were founded, the RR Club of Western Canada, the Canadian RR Association and the RR Club of Eastern Canada. The Eastern and the Western clubs are still active. In addition, ties are growing constantly stronger with the big American clubs south of the border.

Therapy Dog and Ch. Heronhill's Skukuza –
a Ridgeback who has brought comfort and
companionship to many.

Photo courtesy: RRC.

Tracking is a favourite activity with
Ridgebacks. Heronhill's Kumba ROM-
Tracking, is a Canadian example of
broadening the activities with the breed.
Photo courtesy: The Canadian RR Club.

The Eastern club celebrated its 20th anniversary in 1997 and has over 100 family memberships. True to the broad Canadian interest in Ridgeback keeping, the club decided to mark this anniversary with a family picnic event, including Lure coursing, Agility and all kinds of games targeting the pet owner, rather than the show contingent. Over 50 dogs turned up, and the club could also note that the temperaments shown were good. It has now been decided that this should be an annual event with a professional judge critiquing the dogs present.

The Eastern club publishes a newsletter, *The Ridgeback Roster*, four times a year. It covers events, HD results, breed articles, illustrations and it also carries advertising. The club runs a rescue service for Ridgebacks in distress or needing relocation.

Judging by the number of Ridgebacks shown in Canada it is easy to conclude that the breed is in an upward trend. By 1997 many Ridgebacks had achieved Group placings. Despite the tragic and untimely death from cancer of the Am. Can. Champion Crosswick's Integrity, he still topped the list when that year neared its close. Nature is sometimes both unfair and fair. His son, Ch. Rindurr's Kmili Kweli, who went Puppy Best in Show, became a Champion at seven-and-a-half months!

On the increase is also the great Canadian interest in Racing, Lure Coursing, Agility, Obedience and Tracking. Even if the extremes of weather can hamper outdoor activities, the Canadians continue to do more and more with this versatile breed. Two Ridgebacks, Champions Heronhill's Wind Wakker and Heronhill's Yuranga have competed in the Iron Dog Triathlon. This is a three-day event, which includes straight racing, oval racing and lure coursing. The first time either of the above-mentioned two bitches competed at this level, they both finished with top honours.

Several Ridgebacks have been used as therapy dogs and now two have their St John Ambulance Therapy dog certificates. Ridgebacks make surprisingly good therapy dogs with their calm disposition and quiet acceptance of much patting and petting. The residents look forward to their weekly visits and are fascinated by their ridges. The dogs in return look forward to these visits to their friends, who reward them with treats for their good behaviour – and what Ridgeback would not put on its best behaviour for the chance of a little treat? This breed is certainly, as the old saying goes, bribable but incorruptible.

Every dog lover, not least Ridgeback people, should make a note of this Canadian example of canine and human companionship. In a world where the fair rights of dogs and dog ownership are more and more under threat, a bold and systematic presentation of the multiple benefits of keeping and using our dogs in society are our only chance of maintaining a worthy environment for dogs in the third millennium. As an example of campaigning for dogs, a Swedish KC task force, of which I am a part, has even started regular public advertising campaigns to emphasise the beneficial effects of dogs to society. No doubt everyone can learn a lot from Canada!

USA

With the largest population in the developed world, 260 million inhabitants, plus the most dynamic economy, the United States holds a very special position in all aspects of society. The canine world and the Ridgeback world are no exceptions. The American Kennel Club is not a member of the FCI and it has American versions of Breed Standards. In my opinion, it is most important that the American Ridgeback remains under the global umbrella – perhaps hosting an American World Congress – and that the US scene continues to follow the traditions, as well as the Standards, that spring out of Africa.

DOG SHOWS OF THE FUTURE

Dog shows, just like everything else in the US, are magnificent, big and exceptionally competitive. The commercial aspects of

Two classic Ridgebacks heads: Shangara's Mukuru of Samara (above) and Shangara's Mugori of Samara, both Show Champions.

Photo courtesy: P. Rosman.

American Ridgebacks are sometimes, though not always, slimmer and more long-necked than South African, Australian or European brothers and sisters of the breed. This young female, Samara's Ruvanda, is long in body, feminine, with sound muscles and showing good bone.   Photo courtesy: P. Rosman.

One of the classics in US Ridgebacks, which have proven world leadership in versatility, was Ch. Latifu of Shadyridge, a superb Obedience dog also making it in both US and Canadian show rings. This is a dog with great overall balance and excellent angulation.   Photo courtesy: U-B. Ekengren.

canine sports in the US result in formats that the European continent can hardly imagine. Therefore it is necessary for non-American Ridgeback owners, as well as other dog friends, to study the US scene, to admire all the good things and to learn from them. We must view the US system with open eyes, judging what we want to copy and what we want to avoid.

As an example, in the US, points can be scored towards a Championship at thousands of shows, all around this vast country. Therefore showing intensity is a decisive factor, and, consequently, money again plays a major role. Professional handlers dominate the American shows. You can already see two types of result lists; those for top winning dogs and those for the dogs shown by their breeders/owners themselves. Judges are frequently remunerated according to the number of entries, so controversial or tough judging gets little room in these shows.

On the other hand, few if any shows in the world can match the US shows in organisational excellence or viewing comfort. Huge tents give both colour, shade and rain protection. Even the ritual of photographing the winner alone is refined to perfection. Finals in all-breed shows might sometimes be a lot slower than Europeans are used to. Those hundreds and hundreds of visitors that have queued up for tickets to the Best in Group and Best in Show finals for Westminster, as an example, frequently express amazement at the ceremonial slowness of the showing.

Many organisations, not least the FCI, are looking for new, more media-friendly and more dramatic ways of hosting classic dog shows. Ideas about cameras walking around in the finals, the use of giant TV screens and giving the judges' comments direct to the public were discussed, and partially tested, in the centenary show in the Globen hockey hall in Sweden in 1989. If the present type of dog shows are to survive the digital TV age, the shows must change. I suggest that we might, again, watch the US and learn from them. The Americans have not moved yet. But they will!

USA OVERVIEW

I have chosen to base the US scene on illustrations and longer than usual captions. In addition, there are some 'frescos' of facts as well as anecdotes (*see Chapter Six*), all with a bearing on our breed in general.

The first time Rhodesian Ridgebacks were shown in the US as an AKC recognised breed was in Boston. The year was 1956. One of the enthusiastic spectators was a Swedish-born lady, Ulla-Britt Ekengren (see Finland), who bought her first Ridgeback in 1966. This puppy, who became Ch. Banu of Tawny Ridge, was the foundation of the Shadyridge Kennels in 1961. Shadyridge has since developed to be a household name in the US, excelling in at least two areas; the kennel has successfully broadened its interests and its canine sports from the show ring to Obedience and Tracking, and it has been a key contact point for Ridgeback clubs and events in the "Old World".

Successes include Ch. Mgogo of Shadyridge, the first US Ridgeback to get both a show Championship and a Utility Degree (UD). In 1979 another of Mrs Ekengren's puppies, Asali, became the first Ridgeback to win best Puppy at a Canadian all-breed show and then was the first to take Tracking degrees both in the US and Canada. Two years after the puppy success, Ch. Latifu of Shadyridge (with a full title, in US terminology, reading Am.CD,

An American Champion from the later nineties, Samara's Poshi, an exponent of a fantastic power in the chest, both looking at the prosternum and the depth of the ribcage. Bone in balance, and hock well down. Photo courtesy: P. Rosman.

Ch. Centennial Mt Sun Hunter is a recent US top Ridgeback. The shoulder angulation, a long neck and substantial front lead into a superbly curved ribcage. Photo courtesy: C. Heathcock.

Can.CD, Am.TD, Can.TD) became the first RR male to have Tracking Degrees both in the US and in Canada. He also took the Top Obedience RR title in 1981.

This little listing of early achievements has a clear purpose – to show that Ridgebacks have successfully been used for many purposes in the US. I should also add that Ridgebacks have been used in cougar hunting in the US. Unfortunately, few details are known, and this would be another challenge to the US clubs in building their own Ridgeback identity. Sports such as Lure coursing (the US type is long track) are on a world-leading level in the US. Not only do Ridgebacks love this sport, it is good both for the mental and their physical well-being, and when correctly analysed, offers interesting insights to the Ridgeback's breed-specific behavioural patterns.

A less serious and more youthful canine sport, also tested with American Ridgebacks, is Fly-Ball. This sport has a special attraction for younger dog handlers, and it is both fun and exciting for spectators. This is another area where one should expect that American skills in developing attractive mass media products will provide a new, widely-broadcast, canine sport.

American Ridgeback developments have been closely linked to South Africa in more than one way. Major Hawley, who at one stage in his career was Commander of the South African Police Dog Depot in Quaggapoort, South Africa, and was an important writer on the subject of Ridgebacks, left lasting impressions in the US. The successful 'hobby kennel', as the owners prefer to call it, Samara – which is Shona for 'to admire' – started with stock imported from Mrs Liz Megginson in South Africa. Mrs Megginson was therefore not only instrumental in founding the RR World Congresses but also in sending foundation stock to what was destined to be the largest Ridgeback market in the world. The Samara founder, Dr Pamela Rosman, showed the bitch Greenthwaite Tawara of Shangara to what is reported to be the first South African and American RR Champion. Misty, as she was called, was sired by Shangara's Checheni, the all-time top winning South African Ridgeback.

Another individual, with links to Southern Africa, worth remembering is Bruiser. As always in the canine world, the

Choosing to include Ch. Camelot's Technical Knockout in the book was an easy choice. Placing him under the right headline a bit more difficult: He is a US, South African and Zimbabwe Champion. Clayton Heathcock and Cheryl Hadley have achieved the dream of any Ridgeback owner, to prove the quality of their dogs in the home countries of the breed.
Photo courtesy: Barbara Sawyer-Brown.

A bitch that radiates energy as well as muscular strength. But still the female's elegance is uncompromised. Ch. Kwetu Ruffian's Dark Mirage is a winner in all respects – though during some periods in the history of the breed, the size of white on the chest would have been debated. The fact is this is within limits and should not influence the judgement of a top-quality Ridgeback.
Photo courtesy: Barbara Sawyer-Brown.

One of the great masters of US Ridgeback rings, Kwetu's Luke Blackburn, owned by Mike Szabo, winner of nine Best in Show titles at all-breed shows. Close to 200 breed wins make this one of the all-time best-winning Ridgebacks in the world. A short and simplified comment is masculine power in perfect harmony.
Alverson Photographers.

A Ridgeback male is remarkably stronger and more powerful than the female. This American male, Ch. Rusteau of Kwetu, is a good example of the fact that one must appreciate and award extreme dogs, when the extremes are all positive. 'Rusty' shows strong bone, great length of body and a powerful head, all parts in perfect harmony with each other.
Photo courtesy: Barbara Sawyer-Brown.

formal name is more imposing: Am. RSA. Zim. Ch. Camelots Technical Knockout (Calico Ridge The Warlord ex Deer Ridge Morganna). Bruiser was the first serious show dog of Mr Clayton Heathcock and he ranked among the top three Ridgebacks in the US for no less than three consecutive years, in 1992, 1993 and 1994. This might not, however, be the most spectacular part of a great show career: after having finished his US career, he travelled to South Africa, to be handled by Mrs Janet Wang. In the fall of 1995 he took, between October 28th and November 5th, all five required challenge certificates in five consecutive shows. The year after, Bruiser was the top-ranked Ridgeback in South Africa, and the last year, in 1997, he also became a Zimbabwean Champion. The absolute high point in his adventures in the home countries of the breed came in 1996 at the East London all-breed Championship show, where he won the Hound Group and finished Reserve Best in Show! Returning back home to the US, he still added two more titles to his long merit list.

A VOTE OF THANKS

Last, and very, very far from giving a detailed and comprehensive picture of the US Ridgeback scene, I must mention America's Ridgeback Diplomat, Mrs Barbara Sawyer-Brown – breeder, exporter, speaker, worldwide judge and a person whose entire Ridgeback life has been guided by a warm Ridgeback heart. (When I say US Ridgeback Diplomat, Mrs Ulla-Britt Ekengren should also have been given that title – but Mrs Ekengren is actually Swedish by birth. We also need to honour a true American, Mrs Barbara Rupert, who is another of those

admirable flying diplomats of US RR skills.) Mrs Sawyer-Brown bred Ch. Kwetu Koya's Ruffian (Tripper of Gera ex Kwetu's Koya), born in 1974, who was Best of Opposite Sex at the National Specialty in 1977. At one show Kwetu was the dam of the Best of Breed, Best of Winners, Best of Opposite Sex and Best Puppy, all four top placings in one event. Going a step back in bloodlines, Ch. Kwetu's Koya was Mrs Sawyer-Brown's first homebred Champion; back in 1971, she took a second place in the Hound Group, a very rare success for a Ridgeback in those days.

Ch. Rusteau of Kwetu (Bowfield of Kwetu ex Kwetu Ruffian's Wayward Lass), alias Rusty, was the No. 1 Ridgeback in the US in 1991, in all counting systems. Ch. Kwetu's Luke (Kwetu's Pocket Full of Promise ex Kwetu Ruffian's Dark Mirage) took a record-breaking nine all-breed American Best in Show wins, with 192 Best of Breed wins, presumably an all-time world record.

Ending this patchwork of images and facts from the United States here are some hard facts: Ch. Centennial Mt. Sun Hunter, bred by Cathrine and Kevin Harvey was a recent Top Fifty winner. Number two to him was Ch. Filmmaker's Never Surrender of FM, bred by Kate Graham and Cindy Lane; and third place went to Ch. Tahoe's Red October, bred by Sandy Sail, Frank Dipole and Ken Slinks. Ch. Masai's African Genesis, bred by John F. Rodgers was Best of Breed in an RRCUS National Specialty show. Filmmaker's Never Surrender FM has been the leader in the US show list.

The leader in the Obedience competition was Ch. Wheatridge's O B Joyful O'Kahlu (P.Brunstetter/K.Stein).

These three Ridgebacks show what good stud dogs are all about: Kwetu's Luke Blackburn (left) with one of his Best in Show winning sons, Kwetu's Dude of LeCreme, and another son with group winner merits, Veedaven's sir Lancelot.   *Ashbey Photography.*

This is to pay tribute to the absolute winners. The fact is that ending up on the US lists in general takes a lot, considering the size of the Ridgeback population. One should also salute all those who have not been mentioned but who have done well. The eager reader can only get one piece of advice regarding the US – if you are interested in this country, become a club member and see for yourself. Alternatively, use the superb Internet services of the US Ridgeback club.

MEXICO, CENTRAL AND SOUTH AMERICA

We know for a fact that Ridgebacks have existed for years in Mexico. The proximity to the US makes supply an easy matter. There have even been Swedish exports to Mexico. The national Kennel Clubs also note that some Ridgebacks exist in Argentina, Brazil and Colombia, but no attempt to contact local breeders has so far been successful.

SOUTHERN AFRICA

The early history of the Rhodesian Ridgeback, and the events which led to the production of a Breed Standard, point towards treating Southern Africa as one entity.

At the founding meeting of the modern Rhodesian Ridgeback club in the early twenties, Francis Richard Barnes produced a first draft for a description of the breed, based on the best feature of each of the dogs presented, according to notes made at the time by a Mr B.W. Durham. In the newspaper *The Farmers' Weekly* on September 21st 1927 an "Official

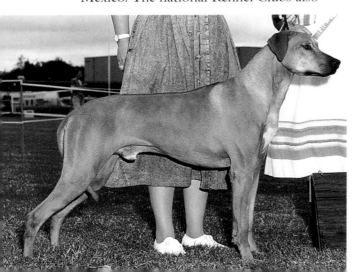

This proudly upstanding male is given the honour of representing Mexican Ridgebacks. The dog, Mr & Mrs Joe Berger's Ch. Rob Norm's Diamond Jim Brady (Kwetu's Pocket Full of Promise/Rob Norm's Sophia Loren) is a solid American Champion, but also a Mexican Champion. The Mexican scene has so far been dominated by imports, and above all, by visiting US dogs 'stealing the shows'. Note the magnificent front and the hind angulation.

Photo courtesy: Mr Berger.

description of the Rhodesian Ridgeback (Lion Dog)" was published. Some eight years later Hutchinson's *Dog Encyclopaedia* printed that same Standard. This original breed description, or Standard, seems to have survived until the mid-fifties. A Ridgeback club formed in 1946 in the Transvaal adopted a Standard with some slight modifications to the original one.

In 1949 the allocation of the breed changed from the original Gun Dog Group to the Hound Group. Then in the late nineteen-fifties came a debate about height and weight. This leads us to believe that there has never been one absolute truth about the detailed conformation of a Ridgeback and that there has always been more than one player in the discussion and development of the breed.

The Rhodesian Ridgeback Club in present-day Harare dates its history back to 1922, to that first meeting of Ridgeback enthusiasts. The Kennel Union of Southern Africa dates the formal foundation of the club to 1924. The club was originally born in Bulawayo, but it moved in 1931 to Salisbury – now Harare. After independence and the name change from Rhodesia to Zimbabwe, in April 1980 the Rhodesian Ridgeback, in the home country of the oldest club, became the Ridgeback. The club in Harare is today seen as the Parent Club and forms a valuable focal point for Ridgeback interest around the world. The entire world of Ridgebacks is indebted to a Sammy and Margaret Wallace, who for decades have guided and advised any club, Ridgeback owner or enthusiast with their enormous experience.

In 1946 the then commander of the South African Police Dog Depot in Quaggapoort,

One of the great examples of solid South African breeding, Ch. Cartouche Unyana (Shangara Sabhuku/Cartouche Samantha), seen here winning Reserve Best of Breed under one of the top US judges, Mrs Barbara Rupert. Note the exceptional elegance in the neck, which makes the bitch not only look elegant, but possibly also taller than she really is. Photo: Stig G. Carlson.

A male reaching the upper limits of the Standard might sometimes be heavy. This example, Cartouche 'Amish, proves that a tall male can be exceptionally elegant. The long slender muscles and a superb neckline add to the overall impression of a capacity of high speed.

167

Captain (later Major) T.C. Hawley, the author of a book on Ridgebacks published in 1957, formed a Rhodesian Ridgeback Club in the Transvaal. In January 1946 the Kennel Union in South Africa, SAKU, noted in its publication that it was understood that a Ridgeback club had been formed in Johannesburg. The history archives of the Kennel Club in Cape Town, one of the keepers of Southern African traditions and facts both for Ridgebacks and for canine development in general, noted that a Ridgeback club was founded in Kenya in 1951. Although Kenya, geographically, is part of East Africa, not Southern Africa, there is no doubt that their game reserves and old hunting lodges would, if they could speak, add a lot to our understanding of ridged dogs.

The Kennel Union of Southern Africa shows a Ridgeback on its emblem. This symbol, known as "The Dog on the Rock" was inspired by a drawing of two Ridgebacks in Hutchinson's *Dog Encyclopaedia,* third volume, by the artist Mrs Sheila Scott Langley. The design was registered, many years later, as the offical and protected symbol for kennel activites in South Africa. In heraldic terminology the symbol is described, in 1984, as "On a circular background Azure, upon a rock, a dog standant gardant Argent".

Measured even by today's standards, the first half-decade from the formal start-up of the breed club, be it in 1922 or 1924, was impressive. The first Ridgebacks, interestingly registered as Steekbaards, entered a show in Bulawayo in 1925 with no less than 24 entries. Many a club starting today sees fewer entries. During the period 1924 to 1930 over 170 Ridgebacks were registered in Southern Africa. During the 1990s in the Republic of South Africa the annual registration numbers of Ridgebacks varied from about 450 to over 800 puppies a year. The Ridgeback is the tenth most popular breed in South Africa. Interestingly, it is the second most exported breed in the country, which gives a clear indication of the quality that prevails in the home countries of the breed. In Zimbabwe the Ridgeback is regularly ranked around number three of all breeds. As a comparison, in the UK, USA and Sweden, three significant Ridgeback countries, the ranking varies between around fortieth and fiftieth place, Australia being some 20 positions higher.

The Southern African scene has also developed a large number of show judges who have always been highly appreciated wherever they have officiated. Names such as Liz Megginson, Sam Wallace and Richard van Aken are familiar in all Ridgeback-friendly parts of the world.

ZIMBABWE

While there have been difficult times for the Rhodesian Ridgeback Club, the Parent Club, notably the period during the Second World War and, more recently, the period prior to and after independence in Zimbabwe, when membership and interest in the Club and its affairs dropped, the Club has remained in existence and, today, is in a very healthy state, with numerous local and overseas members.

The Zimbabwean show circuit is small, with ten Championship shows being held annually, as well as a number of Open shows and Match meetings. The Parent Club does not hold Championship shows on a regular basis, but does hold its annual

This interesting shot, from the Parent Club archives, shows Ch. Rhodesia Maestro Mozart of Inkabusi in 1963. At first glance one might miss the polish; but, the front is exceptionally strong, the bone in balance and the head very powerful.

Outstandingly elegant bitch, with a neckline that is seldom seen even among the very top winners. Superb angulation, combined with a string front makes this only 11 months old female already look like a true champion. Photo: K. Hawkins.

Trophy show in conjunction with the Sporting Dogs (Hound Group) Championship show in May each year. Ridgebacks have a wonderful history in gaining top honours at this show. However, the Club did hold its own Championship show for the first time ever in 1997, to celebrate the 75th Anniversary of the foundation of the club.

Held in August, this was the highlight of the 75th Anniversary Year and the show attracted a record entry of 72 Ridgebacks for the judge, Mr Jack Selby from the United Kingdom. Dogs were entered from all over Zimbabwe and a number of dogs also made the journey up from South Africa to compete. There were numerous overseas visitors, representing Australia, Israel, America and several European countries, who were able to have a good look at the dogs on show. As well as the show, a parade of 15 Veteran dogs was held to honour the dogs and bitches that had contributed to the strength of the breed today in its home country. A large and very appreciative crowd enjoyed the day's events, which commenced with a champagne breakfast and concluded with an after-show dinner.

A few days later, a small group of visitors were taken on a four-day Historical Trip down to Matabeleland, to trace the early history of the breed. Places of interest visited were: Hope Fountain Mission, where the Reverend Charles Helm, the pioneer Missionary, brought his dogs in about 1875; Weltevreden at Mangwe and Van Rooyen's Rest at Plumtree, two farms belonging to Cornelius van Rooyen, the famous big game hunter, who developed and enhanced the reputation of the breed; and Eskdale Farm at Figtree, where Francis

Zimbabwe Ch. Mushana Panduka, a rather low and strong Ridgeback with good angulation and excellent bone structure.
Photo: L. Costa.

Barnes, the founder of the Parent Club, lived and bred his Ridgebacks. The Peard house in Bulawayo, where the first Ridgeback Club meeting was held in 1922, was also visited.

Not only does this country enjoy the privilege of having the oldest Ridgeback Club in the world, but it also had the first Best in Show winner at an all-breeds Championship show. On March 27th 1956, Copper of Ballyboden won Best in Show at the Matabeleland Canine Association all-breeds Championship Show, under judge Mrs Will Judy from the USA. The dog was born on April 8th 1953, sired by Glenwood Leo from Grandridge Judy. He was owned by Mr M.F. Lane-Joynt of "Ballyboden", Matapos, and bred by Mrs O.C. Milne of Bulawayo. Mr Lane-Joynt has donated to the archives of the Parent Club copies of Copper's subsequent Championship Certificate, the receipt for his purchase, press clippings of the momentous day and a photo. Copper cost 8 guineas which, in

those days, was a high price for a dog, but Ridgebacks were much sought after and breeders had no difficulty in selling their pups. Ch. Copper of Ballyboden and his family later moved to Chipinge in the low veldt and he died in the bush in 1961 as bravely as he had lived.

CLASSIC ZIMBABWEAN RIDGEBACKS
The present-day dogs are descended from some marvellous ancestors that have provided a unique foundation for the continuing strength of the breed in Zimbabwe. It would be impossible to name them all, but a few are listed as being particularly noteworthy. Many top producers were never shown; it has always been the good fortune of the breed in this country that show performances have not counted greatly in the selection of breeding stock. Many breeders have been folk who have appreciated qualities of character and strength as well as physical attributes. We are grateful to those breeders who, in their wisdom, bequeathed us such wonderful genetic material to work with today. Surely it is no less our duty to them and to our breed to continue in their productive endeavours?

Janet Murray's book *The Rhodesian Ridgeback 1924-1974* is an extremely comprehensive manual when it comes to seeing pictures and tracing the parentage of some of the early dogs that make up our stock today. There are a few more dogs that we would like to include as having made notable contributions to the breed since then and that may not have been included in previous literature.

Ch. Maestro Mozart of Inkabusi was owned and bred by Mrs Irene Kingcome,

A powerful bitch, with the front, bone, neck and muscles all in harmony. Ch. Mushana Touchwood represents the successful late eighties in Zimbabwean breeding. A full brother to 'Woody' was exported to Denmark.

Photo courtesy of the Parent Club.

Inkabusi. When mated to Mpani's Ilala of Goromonzi, Ch. Mpani's Rip of Colemore was produced. He in turn produced Ch. Mpani's Tsiga of Inkabusi, Chipinga of Mpani and Ch. Etosha of Mpani, among many other very fine dogs. Tsiga went on to produce Ch. (SA) Mpani's Chimombe, used in the foundation of Dr Steph Potgieter's Pronkberg line.

Ch. Mindemoya's Tendella of Inkabusi, also owned by Mrs Irene Kingcome, bred by Mrs Prichard, Mindemoya: when mated to Ch. Maestro Mozart of Inkabusi, Golden Pandora of Inkabusi was produced, who, in turn, produced Ch. Mushana's Fiona, the foundation bitch of the Mushana line.

Mrs Kingcome bred a number of other fine Ridgebacks, notably Ch. Celetebe of Inkabusi, Hell's Angel of Inkabusi and Ch. Cleopatra of Inkabusi, and they have all laid the foundation for many outstanding lines,

including the Mpani kennels of the late breeder and author Mrs M. Arsenis. Mrs Kingcome seems to have obtained most of her stock from Miss M. Welling's Leo Kop kennel: one of the foundation sires for Inkabusi was Ch. Inkabusi's Malo of Leop Kop. Mrs Kingcome's husband was a veterinary surgeon who wrote one of the first scientific descriptions of the dermoid sinus. This document is held in the National Archives of Zimbabwe.

It is somewhat surprising that, in the past, little credit seems to have been given to Mrs Kingcome and her Inkabusi Ridgebacks, but there is no doubt that credit is due.

Other dogs that have contributed significantly to the breed include Ch. Mushana's Fiona, Ch. Glenaholm Lady Muck of Mushana, Ch. Lord Sam, Ch. Mushana Starr Jameson and Ch. Mutongi.

Up until 1986 all registrations of Rhodesian and later Zimbabwean Ridgebacks were processed by KUSA (Kennel Union of Southern Africa) and after then, by the newly formed Zimbabwe Kennel Club. Sometimes it is confusing to trace the ownership, or the breeder, of an individual dog, as the kennel names and prefixes were used, up until the mid-seventies, without any real consistency – e.g. Mushana's Fiona was owned by Mrs Margaret Wallace (Mushana), but was bred by Mrs McCosh, who had no registered kennel name. Today, that bitch would be known as Fiona of Mushana. Likewise, the well-known dog Mpani's Rip of Colemore was bred by Mrs Coleman (Colemore) and owned by Mrs Mylda Arsenis (Mpani). More correctly, today he would be known as Colemore Rip of Mpani.

12 RIDGEBACKS AND THE THIRD MILLENNIUM

The geographical distribution of our breed is, as has been shown by the research behind this book, still uneven. We can see the embryonic status of the breed in South America and the Far East as having enormous potential. Or we can take the view that Ridgebacks should seek their own way, finding homes only when that home is right, when the environment and society is right, and when the level of knowledge about dogs in any given country is right.

Latin America is a vast area which is beginning to understand its real values in almost every aspect of society. There is no reason why Ridgebacks could not be part of the Latin American advancement. I wish, however, that the Latin American countries will go through natural, safe developments when building Ridgeback activities and work through a small group of devoted and enthusiastic individuals. Gradually, clubs must be formed when knowledge, and dedication to the origin of the breed, is advanced enough. Breeders become worried when new countries buy show dogs en masse, just to get a canine-based business

going. This is happening, for instance, in Eastern Europe today. In order to move step-by-step, we must hope, for example, that the European Ridgeback clubs, not least the Portuguese and the developing Spanish RR societies, take it upon themselves to build links to Latin America. There is a need for a strong focus on breed-specific education, and both cultural and linguistic links are major assets.

The Far East should be treated with caution. Big money is available in countries such as Japan and so the temptation for Western breeders to access these markets can be significant. Ridgebacks are not show machines and are not suitable for use as part of a canine business. Treating dogs, in general, as "business" is totally alien to the true concept of canine-human relationships. The very essence of canines is their multi-faceted temperament and their links to their origins. Without taking a negative stance towards the Far Eastern societies, I still must urge caution among breeders who might get requests from there, either to buy merited show dogs, or to buy entire litters from merited parents.

The vast majority of the Muslim countries, both in the Middle East and in Africa, have different social structures, different social developments and different values compared to the Western world. Canine companionship, as we know it, rarely exists. I cannot foresee responsible breeding in the Middle East of a dog such as a Ridgeback, which needs so much respect and devotion and the sharing of life-styles, happening within the first century of the third millennium. It is likely that Israel will remain the last bastion of Ridgebacks towards the East. Possibly, just possibly, We might also see positive changes in (Western) Turkey.

When discussing geography, we need to look at the newly emerged free-market economies in Central and Eastern Europe. On the one hand we have seen a very rapid and very responsible start-up of Ridgeback breeding in countries such as the Czech Republic. Old sporting-dog traditions exist all over Central Europe, from Poland down to Hungary. The other side of the coin is that countries that are just emerging from years of political oppression and where average income levels are still low, also pose certain risks. For instance, many an exhibitor at the World Show in Hungary in 1996 was shocked to see the open puppy trading that took place straight from cars parked all around the showgrounds. Fortunately the young clubs in Central European countries such as the Czech Republic and Slovakia, give us hope. The Balkan developments should be monitored with caution, including Greece.

Dog trading in its worst forms still exists even in Europe – and, to be fair, not only in Central and Eastern Europe. Belgium, the home of the FCI, offers the 'services' of huge animal supermarkets. For those interested in importing material from the new markets, please remember that the pedigrees you might obtain in these markets are not always the real thing. The message is that there is potential, and there are skills, but extreme caution must be exercised. The national Kennel Clubs in all of Central Europe, all the way to the Ukraine, are solid and helpful, and everyone should always engage in a dialogue with them before exporting, or importing, any dog.

THE ETHICAL CODES

The export that the West must make sure reaches every destination is the Ethical Code. It could be the Australian code, which might be the ideal in striking a balance between rules and freedoms, or the British ethics, or the Scandinavian or the Finnish principles – the details do not really matter. The main thing is that the new markets must join Western thinking and live according to these principles. We in the West must understand and remember, though not accept, that in the new European countries attitudes can be different.

For example, a litter of, say, ten Ridgeback puppies, all successfully exported to Germany or Switzerland at German or Swiss prices, might constitute an income, to the seller, equivalent to the salary from a year's work. These realities and temptations do change people's behaviour. This call for caution especially applies to Russia and the former Soviet states.

We should respect the fact that Russia, before the Revolution was, for those times, an advanced country as far as dog sports were concerned. But we must also understand the rules of today's Russia. Quick and big money does exist and the rate at which Russian dog sports are developing raises certain questions. There is a huge rise in the influx of Russian dogs to shows. We know for a fact that Russian breeders are eyeing Ridgebacks. We must hope that breeders in the mature markets pay special attention to possible sales to Russia, and to the implications involved.

The answer is through making personal contacts, interviewing potential buyers and checking with colleagues who might already have contacts and experience. The responsibility is with the mature markets; there is a warm soul in the Russian people, and the general love for companion animals is wonderful. I have, many times, watched how, in the often grey early mornings in the parks around the Kremlin, average Moscovites pour out from the underground stations. They are frequently greeted by homeless dogs of all calibres. It is more a rule than an exception that people share their meagre lunch with these dogs. Among the first literature that was printed by private printers and sold everywhere in street-corner kiosks in the early nineties were dog books. All this proves the point – it is up to us to help, not criticise. That help can only be effective if we understand the conditions that will prevail for some time, and, above all, if we protect our Ridgebacks.

RIDGEBACK NUMBERS AND DEMAND
The problem of popularity is a challenge to which, for instance, both the Australian and Norwegian clubs have given special attention. The Ridgeback is not a beginner's dog and it is not everybody's right choice. Running effective Rescue schemes, such as the ones in the US or UK, is an admirable thing. But it also amounts to curing the results of a problem, not tackling the problem itself. Protective action needs to come ahead of misfortune – which by no means denigrates the valuable work rescue organisations are doing. It is just that we have to focus more on prevention!

There have been suggestions that we should avoid the commercialisation of our breed. This is a noble thought. The problem is that no-one has yet found how to do it. One thing is clear; it is not achieved by keeping silent and not communicating. Silence communicates, but it is unspecific and uncontrolled communication. The best solution so far has been to present the true nature and true demands of the breed. Articles in Kennel Club and general interest magazines, as an example, should honestly and correctly present the breed, not 'sell' it. Literature must be available and it must explain the unique qualities of a Ridgeback. It goes without saying that club bulletins play a pivotal role. It is quality of content and frequency of publication which count, not glossy presentation. And, above all, informative material should be available every time several Ridgebacks are seen together at dog shows! In many countries, fanciers already do this and do it well. This form of activity must be ongoing. It does not demand enormous amounts of money. It takes doing – time after time and year after year. Examples of good articles published, with limited budgets, come, for instance, from France. In many countries, for example Germany, you can obtain small leaflets about the breed at shows – which leads me to the next topic.

GLOBAL CO-OPERATION

The current exchange of ideas and material is a must. Running canine clubs is a rewarding but also a time-consuming hobby. The more every club around the world can avoid reinventing too many wheels, and the more good information material and great ideas can be exchanged, the better the clubs spend their time.

The rapid moves towards new interactive media, such as the Internet, provide technical opportunities to exchange material that have never existed before. We must, however, realise that not all countries have good Internet coverage. In some cases, technology reaches the 'elite', but not the up-and-coming people. Therefore this wonderful new technique, putting the consumer in the decision-maker's seat, should be used, but should not be mistaken for the one and only solution. In time we will have to discover a way of identifying who and what on Internet is serious and professional. At the moment we have two extremes: we have the world leaders in a particular subject talking – and a lot of real crack-pots.

In the 1980s a number of Ridgeback enthusiasts dreamed about a global Ridgeback 'Chapter'. The Danish Ridgeback breeders Pia and Allan Schrattenholtz spent enormous time, for some years, on keeping up a world chapter news bulletin. The amount of labour involved in this endeavour made it, in the end, impossible to continue. Now, with

the professional level that many Ridgeback clubs have reached, we can see a natural task that can be given to each country which undertakes to host the World Congresses – to organise a Global RR 'Chapter', that is an information exchange bank, on the Internet. This should be undertaken for four years, until the next World Congress host country takes over.

THE BREED STANDARD

This has recently been modified by a team from Southern Africa and it has been adopted by the FCI. The content has not changed; communication has. While there is still some lack of clarity in some details, it is the best breed description yet. In general, Breed Standards, for any breed, are written by dog enthusiasts and experts, and very seldom by communications professionals. What we must hope for is a global understanding that a breed can have one, and only one, Standard. Any attempt to rewrite the content of the Rhodesian Ridgeback Standard must be opposed by all available means.

EDUCATION AND RESPECT

All successful societies, all successful corporations and all successful sports are built on these three principles. Whether we view the canine hobby and canine companionship as a part of society or as a part of sport is up to each dog owner. I suggest that if we do not see the social role of the dog as being first and foremost functional, and the sports aspects as icing on the cake, we might not focus enough on the need for defending the rights of the dog in our society. Again, societies vary, and each country must assess its own opportunities and its own threats.

What is of the utmost moral importance is how Ridgeback owners – and all dog lovers – organise themselves. There is a responsibility for the older and more experienced to educate the younger. This is part of our debt to the Ridgeback as a breed.

Each canine organisation that administrates activities and events, be they sports, social events, training, registration and statistics, etc., also has an obligation to keep up an optimal inspiration and motivation level among the dog owners. This assumes that no club should develop only into an elitist sports club. The backbone of the breed, the guarantee that there are enough good homes for our present and future Ridgebacks, is with the common dog-lover. He or she is worth exactly as much as any super show-handler when it comes to taking care of our breed.

The positive development, the work to breed good dogs which have the correct temperament and which conform to the Breed Standard, comes from breeders who have been given both education and inspiration. Success comes from individuals and their ambitions and dreams. Dreams come from an environment of respect. Let us hope that there will never be a Ridgeback world where administrators and rigid rules take over and the importance of the individual dwindles.

TRUE RIDGEBACK TEMPERAMENT

This is the hallmark of the breed and is just as important as the physical conformation and the ridge on the back of the dog. We have no right to change this characteristic – either because 'it would fit better into today's society', or because 'it makes the dog easier to show', or because 'that is how the majority of the Ridgebacks are today'.

There is only one road to a sound future for the Ridgeback as a breed and that is by going back to the dog's origins. The understanding of the true breed idea is both the past and the future. In my view we will never have enough people who have the ability to spend time, energy, money and a major part of their personal ambitions in keeping up the ties to Southern Africa, if Ridgebacks become too popular. Making compromises in order to develop the breed faster is treason. Let us instead see this as a particular dog for particular people. Or, to quote the closing words of Rosy Brook-Risse at the UK World Congress: "Hopefully the Rhodesian Ridgeback will never become a fashion dog. It should always remain a very special type of dog for people who will treasure the very special character of our Ridgeback, a fascinating member of the family."